And The Final Answer Is ... ?

Reflections of a Retired Theologian/Pastor

BY
WILLIAM P. ANDERSON

CARTOONS BY
RICHARD L. DIESSLIN

DIESSLIN PRESS

DAYTON

And The Final Answer Is ... ?

Reflections of a Retired Theologian/Pastor

Author: William P. Anderson
Illustrator: Richard L Diesslin

Diesslin Press : Dayton

ISBN: 978-0-9848872-7-9

Contents

Foreword

The title for this modest work, *And The Final Answer Is … ?*, noticeably lacks an answer. The reason for this is simple. There is no *definitive* answer for the process of theological reflection since exploration is always on-going. There is no way for anyone to exhaust the *infinite*. In this regard, I am following the *a priori* theological principle of St. Anselm of Canterbury, namely, *fides quarens intellectum*, i.e., faith seeking understanding. It is an exciting task, one filled with wonder, awe, and inspiration. The results of this task can be very informative, enlightening and fulfilling.

I have chosen, in these brief writings, to offer some reflections on the idea of God; the person of Jesus of Nazareth, the Christ; the nature of being human; and the problem of evil. In this context, I also offer some reflections on the death and resurrection of Jesus of Nazareth with most of the materials in this domain having their origin in Lenten homilies which I have delivered over the many years of my ministry. The *Seven Last Words* of Jesus from the cross are some of the most powerful words in Christian literature and offer an example of the extent to which I believe our God will go to demonstrate His infinite love. These reflections, however, are not to be considered exhaustive, but simply illustrative of the tasks we have before us.

The texts also include some poetic offerings on these same topics and, as usual, some cartoon illustrations are offered to not only *enlighten*, but also to add a *touch of lightness* and humor, as we wrestle with some difficult and perplexing human issues. For this I am indebted to my former graduate student and now longtime literary colleague, Rich Diesslin, who masterfully offers insight and wit while shedding light on many of these problematic issues.

And so I leave these reflections to you in order that in some small way you may find them useful in exploring these topics in your own life. It is a wonderful experience and I hope you find it so as well.

As always,
Pax et Caritas (Peace and Love)
William P. Anderson, Sr.

Part I - Reflections on God and Faith

1. The Idea of God

Although this is the first chapter in this little book of reflections, it was nevertheless the last one written. It may seem a bit strange, but this reflection was put aside as reflections were being made about Jesus of Nazareth's humanness, ethics, the problem of evil and an assortment of other issues. It is, however, what Origen of Alexandria, the great creative thinker of the early church, would have described as *first principles*. And so, it is both incumbent and necessary for me to now turn to this fundamental issue, to wit: the proposition that the very *idea* of God is the *sine qua non*, the one principle upon which all the other thoughts and reflections are based.

As I began to reflect and put pen to paper, so to speak, I was reading some excerpts from Walter Isaacson's work on Albert Einstein, in particular the great physicist's view of God. While Einstein was not a traditional theist neither was he, by his own testimony, an atheist. Perhaps he can be considered a deist, as he himself declared, and as is the case for many others in the various disciplines of the sciences. And here I think of the notable University of Washington geologist, David R. Montgomery, author of: *The Rocks Don't Lie* and *Dirt* to cite just two examples of his work. But let us hear what Albert Einstein himself has to say on the subject, as quoted by Isaacson: The question put to Einstein was simply: Do you accept the historical existence of Jesus? And his answer was: "Unquestionably! No one can read the Gospels without feeling the actual presence of Jesus. His personality pulsates in every word. No myth is filled with such life." And then the "ultimate" question: Do you believe in God? And his answer was: "I am not an atheist. The problem is too vast for our limited minds. We are in the position of a little child entering a huge library filled with books in many languages. The child knows someone must have written those books. It does not know how. It does not understand the languages in which they were written. The child only dimly suspects a mysterious order in the arrangement of the books but doesn't know what it is. That it seems to me, is the attitude of even the most intelligent human being toward God. We see the universe marvelously arranged and obeying certain laws but only dimly understand these laws."

He elaborates further on the origin of his ideas with the following well-known and often quoted statement - a statement of great insight and value: "Imagination is more important than knowledge. Knowledge is limited. Imagination encircles the world."

In 1930 Einstein composed a brief credo entitled: *What I Believe* in which he attempted to express his deepest feelings clearly and simply for those who were looking for an answer to this eternal and often perplexing question. The following paragraph, cited by, Isaacson (page 387) sums up his view: "The most beautiful emotion we can experience is the *mysterious*. It is the fundamental emotion that stands at the cradle of all true art and science. He to whom this emotion is a stranger, who can no longer wonder and stand rapt in awe, is as good as dead, a snuffed-out candle. To sense that behind anything that can be experienced there is something that our minds cannot grasp, whose beauty and sublimity reaches us only indirectly: this is religiousness. In this sense, and in this sense only, I am a devoutly religious man."

Einstein's statements evoked much discussion and even inspiration,

1. The Idea of God

but, as we might expect, it did not satisfy those of a more dogmatic, doctrinal mind, who were looking for an answer "Yes" or "No." They were seeking an unequivocal *Yes* which he was unable to give---and I will add, rightly so. I have always been a strong advocate of St. Anselm's well-known, but not nearly as often pursued, thesis that religious faith is always a journey toward the unknown, the mysterious. This, I consider, to be the meaning behind his famous principle: *fides quarens intellectum* or as he described it with an alternate wording, i.e. *credo ut intelligam-* -translated as: *faith seeking understanding* and *I believe in order that I may understand*, respectively. This is, in my view, the way of religious thought, the way of theology, the way of faith. If I actually *know* something, I do not have to *believe* it is so, I will have knowledge that it simply is!

Oddly enough, however, Einstein did offer a more detailed explanation to this question as posed to him by a sixth-grade New York City Sunday School student, when she asked him if scientists pray. His basic response was a simple *No*, but that did not necessarily preclude the existence of an *Almighty*. As Einstein went on to explain: "Everyone who is seriously involved in the pursuit of science becomes convinced that a spirit is manifest in the laws of the Universe---a spirit vastly superior to that of man [sic], and one in the face of which we with our modest powers must feel humble. In this way the pursuit of science leads to a religious feeling of a special sort, which is indeed quite different from the religiosity of someone more naive."

Einstein's views were obviously not comforting to everyone. Nevertheless, I find them quite useful and, at the same time, find a correlation with the views of some very prominent and influential theological writers, such as Rudolf Otto in his work: *The Idea of the Holy*, written in 1917 or the work of Rene Descartes in his *Third Meditation*. (*Meditations on First Philosophy*, p. 390) For Otto this experience is an *existential* encounter, whereas for Descartes, it is *rational*, i.e. intellectual affair. For those who are interested, I would suggest they read *The Third Mediation* of Descartes and the wonderfully mystical work of Rudolf Otto.

In light of the foregoing observations, and it is always somewhat comforting to be able to cite Albert Einstein as an ally, I believe we can make some valid suggestions regarding both God and the idea of God." The question of the origin of religion and/or the origin of the idea of God has always been fascinating to humankind, as we human beings stand in awe of this majestic, mysterious, and fascinating cosmos. And this idea of God, and the origin of the idea, is an exciting, fascinating, awe-inspiring task to which we are called. The theologian, William Calloley Tremmel, in his work on religion, analyzes several different origins of religion, including the primitive, the sociogenetic, the psychogenetic, and finally the theogenetic. Although each of these discussions is noteworthy and fascinating in its own way, I am fascinated by the theogenetic hypothesis.

Many theologians and philosophers prefer the more historically verifiable approaches such as we find in the first three analyses presented by Tremmel; nevertheless, there is a long-standing, and I believe valid, approach in the theogenetic perspective origins, some of which may be found, for example, in the writings of Augustine of Hippo, from the late fourth and early fifth centuries, John Calvin in the sixteenth century, and Renee Descartes in the seventeenth century. To illustrate briefly:

> 1. Augustine writes in the preface to his Confessions: "Great are you, O Lord, and greatly to be praise ... you have made us for yourself, and our heart is restless, until it rest in you."

1. The Idea of God

2. This view is consistent with that of Calvin who writes in his magnum opus: *The Institutes of the Christian Religion*: "God himself, to prevent any man from pretending ignorance, has endowed all men with some idea of his Godhead, the meaning of which he constantly renews and changes."

In a slightly different more rational and philosophical manner, Renee Descartes suggests in his *Third Meditation* that our knowledge of God and the very idea of God is innate. That is: it has been placed there by God himself. Here he is following an axiom of the great philosopher, Aristotle, when he maintained the idea of God could not be present there had it not been placed there by God himself.

Descartes states his case in the following manner: "It is obvious ... there must be at least as much reality in the total efficient cause as in its effect, for whence can the effect derive its reality, if not from its cause ... And from this it follows, not only that something cannot be derived from nothing, but also that the more perfect - that is to say, that which contains in itself more reality - cannot be a consequent of the less perfect."

While Descartes point of view is stated in substantially different terms than the religious narratives of scripture, it does, from a rational point of view, make a reasonable case for the origin of the idea of God. However, like Anselm's view of God, Descartes' view is also the God of the philosopher, the fascinating God of speculation and cognition. Nevertheless, I find the suggestion intriguing, and one which invites us all into the realm of mystery, fascination, and awe.

Mircea Eliade, a noted, well-respected theologian and historian of religion, along with other historians of religion, such as Andrew Lang, Nathan Soderbloom and others, seem to agree with this conclusion when they also suggested God, and not humanity is the origin of religion; i.e. faith, the idea of God, and religion is an experience inflicted on humanity from an outside source, namely, from a God out there!

I am suggesting here that people already have and have had, from time immemorial, i.e. back to *primitive* times, the idea of a being who is infinitely perfect. However, nowhere in this world is there anything even remotely perfect that could cause such an idea, nevertheless, the idea is real; it is present. Consequently, it must have come from God - the absolutely perfect being and must have been imposed from somewhere out there. Of course this is the God of the philosophers like Descartes, Anselm and others, who for many (perhaps even most believers) does not seem to measure up to the God of Abraham, Jesus, Gautama Buddha or Mohammed, *et al.*

Enter Rudolf Otto! This is where Otto's view of God comes into the picture. For Otto, religion is not something invented *by* humans, but rather something given *to* humans. However, unlike Descartes, whose view of God is far to rational for Otto, religion or religious faith is predominately a *feeling* aroused by the impact of a "sense of awe," "a sense of holiness," or as Otto's predecessor, Friederick Schleiermacher put it: *gefuhl*, a "feeling of absolute dependence." In these latter statements, there is in humans an awaking, an awareness of "createdness," of "finitude," instilling in us an awareness of the "mysterious Holy Other." For this experience Otto creates a new term: namely, the *"numinous!"*

1. The Idea of God

Theologian Rudolph Otto Looks at the Universe

This mysterious and tremendous feeling is described by Otto in the following way: "[...] like a gentle tide, pervading the mind with a tranquil mood of deepest worship [...]. It may burst in a sudden eruption from the depths of the soul with spasms and convulsions, or lead to the strangest excitements, to intoxicated frenzy, to transport, and to ecstasy. It has its wild demonic forms and can sink to an almost grisly horror and shuddering ... again it may be developed into something beautiful and pure and glorious. It may become a hushed, trembling, speechless humility of the creature in the presence of - whom or what? In the presence of that which is *MYSTERY* inexpressible and above all creatures." (*The Idea of the Holy*, pp. 12-13) (emphasis added)

To summarize this brief excursion into a view of the *theological origins of religion*, let me just state, clearly and unequivocally: the *idea* that

God is a *given.* Therefore in all that follows, I am presuming the very existence of an infinite being, or spirit - to use Einstein's words - as the fundamental foundation for all that I say. Obviously, the *infinite* cannot be demonstrated empirically, or scientifically. However, neither can science dispute the infinite for its speculations would be no more valid than my own. Both, however, have legitimate roles to play in the development of human life with all of its avenues of exploration, speculation, and application and each can contribute to the betterment of this rather difficult, hostile world in which we find ourselves.

Having said this, let me close with this personal experience. In the Fall of 1968, shortly after I joined the faculty of theological studies at the University of Dayton, I was invited by the Chair of the Department of Philosophy to be part of a panel to field questions from the University Faculty Wives Club. I was invited, I am almost certain, because I was a liberal Protestant theologian teaching at a Roman Catholic University, under the auspices of the Society of Mary. I was invited to join the theological faculty, in a very exciting "Post-Vatican II theological world," along with several other Protestant scholars in a variety of disciplines, e.g. Science and Religion, Hebrew and Greek studies, including exegesis, etc., to develop a graduate program in theological studies and pastoral ministries.

At the very outset of the evening's program, one of the faculty wives addressed the following question to me. Simply put, she asked: "Dr. Anderson, would you *define God* for me?

My response was the following: The meaning of the *word* God is that it has *no meaning,* but that it accrues *meaning* in human experience throughout history. *Finitum non capax infiniti!* The finite is not capable

1. The Idea of God

of knowing or defining, the infinite! This was Einstein's view; it was Otto's view; it is the view of any rational being including the Apostle Paul who wrote, "Now I see in a mirror, darkly, then (ultimately) I shall see face to face!"

Dr. Richard Baker, the Department of Philosophy Chair, an advocate of the philosophy and theology of St. Thomas Aquinas, remarked after I had responded to the question: "Well, that goes to prove you should *never* ask a theologian - especially a liberal Protestant one, to define God!"

It was, nevertheless, even in light of this rocky, opening question, a very pleasant and enjoyable evening of discussion. It did not, moreover, hinder my career at the university in the least, and we "Protestants" assisted our Roman Catholic colleagues in developing a very fine graduate program. And I spent more than the next thirty years at the University and am currently an Emeritus Professor of Religious Studies, a very nice honor!

Let us now proceed to some of the topics at hand!

2. *The Essence of Faith*

As we celebrate our faith at different but equally significant times of the year, e.g. Advent, Christmas, Lent, Holy Week, from the simple and beautiful story of the manger to the poignant entry of Jesus riding into Jerusalem on a beast of burden, to his trial, beating and death, followed by the joy, grace and love of the resurrection experience, it is incumbent upon us to open our hearts, spirits and minds to the power this faith may have in a world in desperate need today. We should diligently remember these events as the core, the basis, the essence of our faith, as the foundation of our belief and that which gives us hope. We should reach out to all human beings regardless of race, gender, status in, or style of, life. And finally, we must embrace, reach out and care for a world which needs compassion, integrity, and love.

It is never too late, nor is it ever inappropriate, to reflect on these beliefs. We should remember and understand the ancient Anglo-Saxon word, *be-lief* literally means what a person lives by, and so must we. We draw strength from our faith; we discover hope for our lives; we feel the grace and power of a God who surrounds us as we think on all these things. But this is meaningless unless we convert our faith experience into concrete reality, unless we actually live these values as truly and as often as we are able.

We may not be able to accomplish great deeds; our talent and resources may be limited. Nevertheless, let me state clearly: no good deed, no concern for another human being is too small to be pleasing to our God, to be of value in this life, or to go unnoticed by those who see with eyes of faith. The importance of this is made clear in the concluding verse of the Apostle Paul's great *Hymn of Love* in his first epistle to the Christians of Corinth when he wrote these immortal and memorable words: "faith, hope, love abide, these three: but the greatest of these is love."

Demonstrating love, doing good, sharing with those less fortunate are values and principles worth pursuing; they are things of beauty. The great English poet, John Keats, captured this thought magnificently when he wrote these immortal words in his masterpiece, *Endymion:*

2. The Essence of Faith

A thing of beauty is a joy forever;

Its loveliness increases; it will never

Pass into nothingness; but still will keep

A bower quiet for us, and sleep

Full of sweet dreams, and health, and quiet breathing.

Don't Leave Home Without It

Properly understood and lived kindly and gently, the Christian gospel is itself a thing of beauty and joy even to eternity. So, be at peace; do good; share love with all you meet; and the grace of our God shall surround you and the power of this same God shall uphold you; and the love of our God will flow in and through you.

Part I - Reflections on God and Faith

3. God's Insatiable Love

As I sit here in my study at my desk and occasionally peer out the window to catch a glimpse of the beautiful falling snow, so white and clean - glistening in the daylight like sparkling diamonds - it is hard to believe we are, at the same time in the midst of the Lenten Season, a season in which and through which we journey with Jesus of Nazareth on his way to Jerusalem and the cross. The beauty of the snow, together with the spring and summer which shall follow so quickly also remind me of the magnificence of our God, together with the unfathomable depths of our humanness and of lives richly blessed.

At the same time we are existentially aware the journey we are taking with Jesus of Nazareth moves steadfastly toward Jerusalem and the certainty of his death - bringing to the forefront of our minds the evil, hate, corruption, and prejudice which runs rampant in the world we are called upon to serve and love. Clearly it is a difficult, complex world in which we find ourselves - a world which challenges the very essence of our faith. Often, I have asked myself, as I reflect on these issues: am I up to, am I worthy of, such challenges? Like most of us in this world, I am a work in progress. There are times I am truly up to the tasks at hand. There are other times, when clearly, I am not! We are - even with the grace, generosity, and love of our God and the depth of the resources of our humanity - all of us - remain *finite!* Great as we are, or may become, we are limited in our strengths and abilities. Nevertheless, there is one *unalterable factor to be considered:* we are loved - always loved - by a power, grace, and peace far beyond our comprehension. *We see this most clearly in the incarnation of God's love in Jesus of Nazareth!* Is this not the truth in the beautiful parable of prodigal father and his two sons? Surely it is!

Some of my dearest and closest friends are fond of referring to me as an eternal optimist! And in total agreement, my most vocal critics like to add the less honorific term - naive. Thus they see me as a *naive*, eternal optimist. Together they frequently joyfully, gleefully, unite in a critique of my views that is not always so gentle, not always kind, but, at the same time, quite engaging as we pursue the wonder, awe, and mystery of life together.

So then, what can I do or say to these friends and critics? The simple answer is this: I truly and sincerely believe (in the old Anglo-Saxon sense of the term) God is love, that is: *agapeistic* (i.e., other-centered) love. I further believe this love is the ground and source of all that is, all that can and is to be. It is the given and given freely it challenges each of us to reflect not only on the wonder and beauty of creation, but on the *mystery and awe of the One Who gives, the One we call God.*

As some psychologists, such as Erich Fromm and Gordon Allport, have argued, we human beings are in many ways quite unique. They argue, and I concur, human beings, uniquely perhaps, have a capacity for self-transcendence, i.e. human beings have an ability to reach beyond the pale of their limited, finite experience into a world we shall call the *noumenal.* In a fleeting moment beyond space and time, a moment when we have a special perception of how wonderful, how awe-inspiring life can be - even our miniscule, finite lives. In that moment, as we open our hearts, minds, and spirits to the noumenal, we can experience the very essence of God who wishes for us to be people of love, people of grace and mercy, seeing in all: that is, in all races, all cultures, in every life-style, every religion, the beauty and richness of God's own inner being, namely: Love Itself! The late Scottish philosopher/theologian, John Baillie has referred to this as: "The Sense of the Presence of God," in his book by the same title. And, we may add, the Apostle Paul put it simply and succinctly in these well-known words from his second letter to the Christians of Corinth, we he stated: "we become (as it were) 'new beings' in Christ - the old passes away and everything becomes new. We are a 'new creation.'" God is here perceived as the source of all sources, the foundation of all grace and love, the author of all compassion, closer than our next thought, nearer than next breath and the *One* who invites each of us, without reservation or restriction, into the inner circle of love, grace, mercy, peace and truth. We are simply *to accept the fact we*

3. God's Insatiable Love

are accepted! Indeed, 'acceptable' just as we are!

God's Love for Humanity

These thoughts are the foundation of every sermon I have delivered or will deliver; they are the underlying basis of all the theological lectures and presentations I have made or will make, for I consider them to be the essence of the gospel; this is the *agape*-love of which the beloved John so eloquently spoke and wrote. When we experience this love, when we experience this love incarnate in Jesus of Nazareth, when we are able to perceive this love in the eyes, hearts, and spirits of our fellow human beings - without reservation - from the smallest child to the most aged of adults, from the East and the West, from the North and the South, whether they be red, yellow, black, brown, or white, whether they be gay or straight, when we are able to experience this kind of love, then we shall find beauty in life - even in the midst of turmoil, even in the midst of hate, even in those who vehemently oppose us - we shall discover and experience love! Moreover, we shall be empowered to share God's healing with those who are oppressed, hungry, disenfranchised, and in deep need. We shall be fulfilling the challenge of Jesus when he put forth this command to all who follow him: *Inasmuch as you have done it unto the least of these my, sisters and brothers, you have done it unto me!* While this is truly a difficult challenge, I am encouraged by the dedication, faith and love of people such as Mother Teresa who once described what I have been saying here in these simple terms: "Every act of love is peace, no matter how small." Or as Augustine once described the extravagance of the love of God when he said: "God's love is everywhere the 'Center' and with respect to God's love there is no circumference!" These are real, substantial challenges for each and every one of us!

The God of whom I here speak and whom I, in a limited finite way, understand, is known throughout the world by many names. The God I love and experience is simply too big to fit into any one religion, any single religious expression. Most human beings who seek after God do so until the God they seek *finds* them. Augustine put it quite eloquently in his work called, *Confessions*, when he wrote in the preface, "O Lord, our hearts are restless, until they find there rest in Thee!" When an event such as that occurs, they (and we) may know and experience real peace and joy in life.

In light of this, let us do our utmost to be agents of reconciliation and reconciling love. Often-times, as is clear from even a casual look at this world, we forget God, and more importantly, we overlook God's embracing, all-inclusive love right there in our midst. Nevertheless, I take comfort from this simple thought: while we, finite human beings may forget God, God does not, and will not - ever - forget us! God has been,

3. God's Insatiable Love

is and always shall be a God of forgiveness, grace, mercy, and love and will continue to remind us, again and again, reaching out toward us in love - awaiting our response.

So, be at peace and may the love of God in all its extravagance and generosity surround us; may the strength of God and the gentle power of God abide in and through us, allowing the grace of God to flow forth from us reaching out with tenderness and compassion to all the children of God - which simply means: to everyone!

4. Evil and The God of Love

One of the most difficult and, at times, agonizing problems for any believer in God is the so-called *problem of evil.* We wonder, if our God is all we claim that God is, why is so much unnecessary pain, hatred, abuse and misuse of good things a part of human life?

The attempt to justify the power, goodness, justice, and love of God in spite of the evil we experience, and, perhaps, even inflict on ourselves in our human existence, is called a *theodicy.* Moreover, generating a *theodicy* is particularly difficult for adherents of the Judeo-Christian tradition since the Christian faith maintains affirmations about the deity, such as, omnipotence, omniscience, omnibenevolence, which are *incompatible* with the existence or even the possibility of the existence of evil. This would be true not only of Christianity, but any *theistic faith*, e.g. Judaism, Islam. On the other hand, this is not at all a problem for an "atheist" who does not believe in, nor posit, a God and consequently has no need to reconcile the existence of evil in the world with any ultimate being or principle.

Following below are some brief summaries of attempts which have been offered over the centuries to explain the existence of evil in a world created by an all-powerful, all-loving, and all-knowing God. Whether or not they are satisfactory is a matter of opinion or belief - but they are nevertheless interesting and at least in some measure helpful.

Evil as an unreality: this point of view argues evil does not have any substantial reality but is either an illusion or is limited by some other force (e.g., a God?) such as we find in the religious thought of Zoroastrianism or some force such as that which is found in the dualistic philosophy known as Manichaeism. To the Christian faith both of these dualistic positions are totally unacceptable. This amounts to a denial of the omnipotence of God. The point is God's essence is goodness itself and therefore God does not create evil. *Privatio boni* is the term given to describe this position and is advocated by Augustine of Hippo (who said essentially evil can not exist on its own but only as the privation (absence) of good).

The denial of God's benevolence: while goodness and love, *agape*-love (i.e. sacrificial, other-centered love) is especially central to the concept of God in the traditions of Judaism and Christianity, this is not true of all religions. One simply has to take a look at the gods of the Greeks and the Romans to confirm this point. The idea of may gods and the denial of God's benevolence is unacceptable to western monotheistic religious traditions. Thus this idea is rejected!

Karma theories: these theories are found mostly in eastern religions such as: Hinduism, Buddhism, *et al*. The unique feature of this theory is that the idea of cause-and-effect are central. Advocates of this theory, i.e.

4. Evil and The God of Love

Karma, maintain the evil we experience or do not experience is a consequence of our actions and behaviors in this, or a previous, life and we are receiving what we deserve contingent upon the goodness or badness of that behavior. Moreover, our next life will be determined by how much our goodness outweighs the evil we do, i.e. our "bad" karma. As is clear, Judaism, Christianity and Islam all reject the theory of karma as found in eastern religious thought.

Harmony theories: this approach includes a theme of universal harmony, a harmony which is believed to exist in the present but which is unknown to us because of our limited perspectives and/or understanding of reality (perhaps examples of *non capax infiniti*?). Moreover, it is one which will become known in the future like the unfolding of a work art and sculpture - we see it emerging. A marvelous example of this can be seen in the National Art Museum in Florence, Italy, where they have on display, figures emerging, at various stages from the marble, lined up and down the center aisle. These were works chipped away by the great Renaissance artist, Michelangelo, but never finished. The sculptures are at various stages of completion, and the more complete, the clearer and more beautiful. It is a wonderful (and one might argue spiritual) experience simply to view this phenomenon. We are able to see life, reality, and meaning come into being right before our eyes.

Free-will theories: this is a prominent theme in theodicy and one which emphasizes the freedom of the human will. God chooses to create beings who are endowed with free-will. Thus, the possibility of evil is inherent in our freedom of will. The free-will defense forms a part of the theodicies of such notable thinkers as: Friedrich Schleiermacher, C. S. Lewis, and John Hick and, indeed, can be traced back to the early church leader, Irenaeus of Lyons. These thinkers argue, and I believe correctly, the exercise of free-will may account for moral evil, but does not address the problem of natural evil. On this matter, Augustine, i.e. the advocate of the position that evil is a *privatio boni,* an absence of the good, held the view that the sin of Adam and Eve resulted not only in the fall of humanity, but that the order of nature itself was greatly altered as well. John Hick does not subscribe to this view regarding natural evil, by which we mean such things as natural disaster, physical pain, etc., rather Hick, and others such as Irenaeus of Lyon and Schleiermacher, along with the evolutionary humanist Julian Huxley, see natural evil as a consequence of evolution and a natural world, whose environment is one in which our choices have real and significant consequences, e.g. as may be seen in the contemporary debate over climate change.

These themes do not by any means exhaust the possibilities for discussion of the problem of evil - which is one of the most fascinating, as well as difficult, in all of theological discourse. Nevertheless, they are some of the most well-known suggestions that have been offered to reconcile the difficulty that exists in reconciling the idea of God in western religions and the existence of natural and moral evil.

Personally I am an advocate of the free-will theories, not only for the reasons offered above, but also because this position is one in which there can be fruitful dialogue between religious thinkers and the scientific community. This can be observed in the works of people such as Pierre Teilhard de Chardin and Julian Huxley both of whom have strong scientific orientations, but, at the same time, are open to philosophical-theological discussion. In addition, I recently became acquainted with the work of a noted, contemporary geologist, David R. Montgomery,

4. Evil and The God of Love

of the University of Washington who is open to serious dialogue with religious and philosophical thinkers seeing no incompatibility with their separate, but equally significant positions. There is in this view, at least in principle, religious truth and scientific truth, which do not necessarily mutually exclude each other.

The final word on the Christian God of Love and the very real presence of evil in our life experience has not been spoken and perhaps never will. As stated earlier, in agreement with Albert Einstein's point of view, one cannot be confronted by Jesus of Nazareth and/or his teachings and dismiss them as myth. Einstein enthusiastically argues that every fiber of the Jesus experience pulsates with "life-changing" truth. Furthermore, the essence of this experience, dynamic as it may be, is yet a *mystery* too vast to be totally resolved by our finite minds.

Einstein further articulates these views on religion in a brief credo when he states: "The most beautiful emotion we can experience is the *mysterious*. It is the fundamental emotion that stands at the cradle of all true art and science. He to whom this emotion is a stranger, who can no longer wonder and stand rapt in awe, is as good as dead, a snuffed out candle. To sense that behind anything that can be experienced is something that our minds cannot grasp, whose beauty and sublimity reaches us only indirectly: this is *religiousness*."

There are many more quotations which could be cited here, but these shall suffice. I find them enormously consonant with the great mystics of the traditions of many religions. My favorite here, perhaps, is Rudolf Otto with his ideas of the *mysterium tremendum* and the *noumenal*, as well as his notion of *fascinans*.

5. Some Poetic Reflections

PARADOX

Truth, e'er so elusive, though constantly pursued
    in this age of ours;

Beauty, blighted by a disinterested, self-centered,
    society of shallow men;

Love, bandied about in an amoral world, who now
    knows its precious meaning for us?

But still, in tender moments of silence -
    In moments of flight to the Noumenal
        when we listen with our hearts,
        when we feel with our souls,
        when we see with our spirits,

    We all may know!

For Truth, and Beauty, and Love are Everywhere
    waiting to be born!

SELF-TRANSCENDENCE

Nothingness!
        Estrangement!
   Alienation!
Plastic figures torn apart by a World
      Racing unknown toward its own destruction!

How do we resist Leviathan?

  How do we stand against evil in the World?

Fulfillment!

  Harmony!

 Peace!

Sensitive Beings standing at the Abyss with

  Healing Power and Love.

Inner strength from the Fountain of

  the Universe.

A gift of peace and Love from the

  True Light of the World!

THE GIFT

Life's greatest gift is simple, pure and clear,

Always other-centered, bringing light that all may see

And hear the touchstone, the model: Jesus of Nazareth

God's love incarnate: quietly, gently, always near.

Love has no bounds, belongs to no race,

Nation, gender or season; this gift of peace,

Joy and compassion is freely given.

God's Love Incarnate for all - always the reason!

Part II - *Thoughts About Jesus of Nazareth*

1. *Jesus as "The Christ"*
A Brief Historical Perspective

For the Christian faith, Jesus of Nazareth is the center, albeit, the starting-point of faith. At least initially Christianity is not a set of beliefs, doctrines, ethic or an ecclesiastical organization. Rather, the Christian faith and Christianity begins as a response to the person of Jesus of Nazareth himself. Beliefs began when those who responded in faith and became disciples began to reflect upon the meaning and implications of their actions. In this manner both the scriptures we call the "New Testament" and the organization we call the "Church" came into being. These scriptures and the church which have evolved must, therefore, be subjected to the most rigorous testing and criticism in light of the starting point of Christianity - namely, Jesus of Nazareth, the One Who is claimed to be and is called "The Christ."

This very same principle is central for the great protestant reformers of the sixteenth century, e.g. Zwingli, Luther, and Calvin along with many others: *reformata sed semper reformanda* (having been reformed, but "always" being reformed).

Nevertheless, we still ask, who, precisely is this Jesus of Nazareth? To respond simply and directly: Jesus of Nazareth lived within the borders of what today is Israel. He was totally and unambiguously human, by race a Jew, in sex a male, culturally of the 1st century of the Common Era. *The Presbyterian USA's Confession of 1967* stated it this way:

> "In Jesus of Nazareth, true humanity was realized once for
> all. Jesus, a Palestinian Jew, lived among his own people

and shared their needs, temptations, joys and sorrows. He expressed the love of God in word and deed and became a brother to all kinds of sinful men and women. But his complete obedience led him into conflict with his people. His life and teaching judged their goodness, religious aspirations, and national hopes. Many rejected him and demanded his death. In giving himself freely for them he took upon himself the judgment under which everyone stands convicted. God raised him from the dead, vindicating him as Messiah and Lord. The victim of sin became the victor, and won the victory over sin and death for us all." (*The Confession of 1967*, Part I, Section A. 1)

Intellectually this response involves a belief about the "nature" and or "significance of Jesus of Nazareth. For the Christian response sees him and accepts him as "The Christ" (cf. Matthew 16:19). But what does Christ as the distinctive title for Jesus of Nazareth mean? It implies a relation to God, some special connection between Jesus as the Christ and the Godhead.

The ancient creeds which define this relation, those produced by the Council of Nicea in 325 C.E., the Council of Constantinople in 381 C.E., and the Council of Chalcedon in 451 C.E. all offer the formula that Jesus of Nazareth as the Christ, is "of one substance with the Father" using the Greek word *ousia*, which was Latinized as *substantia*. They were asserting Jesus of Nazareth, as the Christ, was *divine* because he was of the same substance as God. The intention of these formulae is clear: there was a total difference between the Creator and the created, between God and humanity. God exists without beginning or end as the sole uncreated, self-existent reality, and everything else exists because God has willed its existence. Accordingly, Jesus of Nazareth, as the Christ, was God incarnate and not simply a supremely good human being, or great prophet, or a religious genius. Thus the councils wanted to assert a unique status for Jesus of Nazareth as incarnated deity.

Early Church Councils - *Inflicting* Orthodoxy

This is, and has for centuries been, the central claim of Christianity about its founder. In later generations other believers have had difficulty in accepting these formulae grounded as they are in the philosophies of the third, fourth, and fifth centuries, and, therefore, have offered alternative views of who Jesus of Nazareth as the Christ, truly is. In general these occurred in the intellectual upheaval that took place in the nineteenth century, particularly in the person of the German Reformed theologian, Friedrich Schleiermacher. Desirous of moving away from the categories of substance which permeate the classical statements about Jesus of Naza-

1. Jesus as "The Christ"

reth, as the Christ, Schleiermacher in his works: *Speeches: On Religion To Its Cultured Despisers*, and in his major treatise, *The Christian Faith*, argues the uniqueness of Jesus of Nazareth in terms of his "God-consciousness." The whole of Christianity is dependent upon the reality of the vision of the divine with the human, both in the person of Jesus of Nazareth and in the vision of the Spirit with the church.

Central to understanding Schleiermacher's understanding of the Christian faith was his understanding of sin and the redemptive work of Jesus of Nazareth. Sin is the experience of our innate "God-consciousness" being hindered by the conflict between our fleshly sensual nature and our higher spiritual nature. Like Augustine before him, he saw sin as a disorder and a confusion of humanity's loves, whereby humans place their love in that which is worldly or temporal rather than in God and the Eternal.

The redemptive work comes only from outside of humanity, from the person of Jesus, as the Christ, by means of his self-communication to human beings of "his unique God-consciousness." Along with the growth of his natural powers and ability, his God-consciousness gained perfect control of his entire person." In this sense, Schleiermacher suggests we may argue that Jesus had sinlessness and perfection, and we can make this claim without any reference to the outdated formulae of the early church. Jesus is best understood as the full historical realization of archetypal humanity, i.e. "the Second Adam," "the true Adam," "the New Creation," "The New Being," of whom the Apostle Paul speaks so eloquently in his Second Letter to the Corinthians. Jesus embodies concretely the new race of humanity and becomes the exemplar of God's will for us. He is the mirror in which we see our true image and measure.

Who's On First?

These are just a few reflections on who this Jesus of Nazareth is in the long history of our theological tradition. They are *theologies* and should be seen in that manner, i.e. not dogma nor even doctrine. The essence of the gospel in my view is very simple: namely, that in Jesus of Nazareth, God's eternal, insatiable *Love* became incarnate and available to each of us. At the same time, it is useful and positive for us to reflect upon this marvelous gift, as did our ancient forbears and our more recent contributors such as Friedrich Schleiermacher. Personally, I am fond of simply saying: "Jesus of Nazareth, the One Whom we claim as the Christ, is the very incarnation of the *Love of God*!"

2. A Christmas Reflection: Fear Not

I am wondering if some of you, like me, feel that this year the seasons of Advent and Christmas with their spirits of joy, hope, and love have come just in time.

In spite of the usual reasons for elated anticipation, our nation is confronted by, and challenged with, frightening issues to its continued existence and finds itself reaching out in hope for wisdom and truth. Our normal confidence and certainty is proving to be unreliable.

The Advent stories bring to us an essential and timely word. Angels tell Joseph, then Mary, then the shepherds "Do not be afraid!" Something amazing, something wonderful, something unexpected is happening, but you do not need to have any fear. Their announcements are an appropriate introduction to the One they announce, who tells his followers repeatedly, "Do not be afraid!"

Do not be afraid, Joseph and Mary, do not fear people will talk about you, gossip about you. Do not be afraid shepherds that people will think you have lost all common sense. Do not be afraid disciples that people will scoff at you or that you will just not know what to say or how to say it.

And do not be afraid you are not worthy of God's abiding presence and interest in the world and *in you personally.* God has plans for carpenters and fishermen and teen-aged girls. God has plans for each and every one of us—including all who hear these words of love and compassion. You see, God *refuses* to be God without us. What is incredible is the idea - the reality - that God chooses to be gracious and loving through us - through you and through me!

I see this in many people every day, as they offer a warm coat or a warm, gentle word to those who rarely receive either. I see this as they invite the unloved and unlovely into their circle of friendship, into their fellowship. I see this as they are inspired and find resources to share - resources they did not even know they had - with music and pageant, and preaching, and grace and compassion and love. And as they do, they carry with them the sum and substance of that same *counter-cultural* word spoken more than two millennia ago - "Do Not Be Afraid!"

Fishers of Men

Even as others continue to build walls of exclusion, erect towers of hate, and fill the lands with floods of evil, may you reach out in love to those too long on the outside: the poor, the weak, the estranged, those who are mistreated and misunderstood in so many ways. Declare publicly and repeatedly no one is outside the grace and love of God! Affirm the God who *is* love does not belong to any one faith, any one denomination, or

2. A Christmas Reflection: Fear Not

any one person. God reaches out to all human beings - this is what this season teaches us - this is the *esse* of the gospel; this is *our raison d'etre*!

We have much work yet to do: in our nation, in our churches, and in God's most beautiful world. Sometimes it can feel so overwhelming. Therefore, how grateful I am as I think of all of you: friends, colleagues, and family, all partners in this journey of life - in the journey we share together. I am grateful for all you *good and gentlefolk*! Hear once again those beautiful sounding words from Jesus of Nazareth, the One Whom we claim as the Christ, "Do not be afraid!"

3. Jesus - The Feminist

I have always considered *feminist theology* to be very much a part of the larger genre known as *Liberation Theology*, made famous by the South American Roman Catholic priest Gustavo Gutierrez and his epoch making book: *A Theology of Liberation* first published in 1973 and then again in 1988. It is my position, which I shall attempt to make clear, that there is no doubt that Jesus of Nazareth, the One we claim as the Christ, is clearly a feminist and is so in a very positive manner.

Of course, by Jesus we are referring to the historical person, a Palestinian rabbi who lived about two thousand years or so ago. When we use the term "feminist," what we mean is a person who promotes, who favors, the equality of women with men, a person who advocates and attempts to practice treating women as human beings as men are so treated and one who willingly and knowingly challenges existing social standards and customs in so acting. Certainly, Jesus of Nazareth did this, as we shall try to demonstrate here.

To achieve this it is incumbent upon us to demonstrate that Jesus neither said nor did anything which would indicate he advocated treating women as being inferior to men on any level, but, on the contrary, that he said and did things which in quite the opposite fashion indicated he considered women as the equal of men and further that in this process he willingly and knowingly violated existing social mores.

A brief survey of the gospel literature will disclose Jesus nowhere treats women as inferior human beings. Rather it can be argued he felt especially called to free the oppressed, who were being treated as inferior human beings, i.e. the poor, the lame, the sinner, and women and to call them to freedom and equality in his kingdom, which begins here in this earthly, secular realm. Two factors are important here: (1) the status of women in ancient Palestine, that is: in the cultural milieu of Jesus of Nazareth and (2) the nature of the gospels themselves.

What may we say of women in the Palestine of Jesus? It seems clear that women were treated as inferiors in spite of the fact there are several so-called heroines in the biblical tradition. For example: women were prohibited from the study of scripture, e.g. the *Torah*. In Jesus' day it was said it would be better for the *Torah* to burn than to have it entrusted to a woman. Moreover, women were so little thought of that they, along with slaves and children, were not obliged to recite the *Shema*, the Morning Prayer, nor the mealtime prayers. The prevailing attitude was such that a man who needed to have his wife or child say grace for him should be cursed. A similar attitude is reflected in the daily prayers of Jews as well: "Praise be to God that he has not created me a gentile; praise be to God that he has not created me a woman; praise be to God that he has not created me an ignorant man!" In my opinion such a statement is the epitome

3. Jesus - The Feminist

of ignorance! Perhaps this is what the Apostle Paul was referring to when he penned these words in writing to the Galatians: "There is neither Jew nor Greek, there is neither slave nor free, *there is neither male nor female* for you are all one in Christ Jesus." (emphasis added)

These statements all referred to private prayers, but women were just as restricted in the public arena, perhaps even more so. Women were not even counted toward the number necessary for a quorum to form a congregation to worship. Once again they were classified with slaves and children. So rigid was the stricture that men were not even to converse with women in public not even wives or daughters. If a man did so it was considered that it brought misfortune upon himself, neglected the law and ultimately earned "hell." A rather steep price for simply speaking with a woman!

It is in the institution of marriage, however, and the surrounding customs of that estate that epitomize the attitude of society toward women in the day of Jesus. Women were thought of in terms of child bearing and rearing; women were always under the authority of a male, either a father or a husband, or if a widow, the deceased husband's brother. Moreover, divorce could be attained by a male merely by giving a writ of divorcement, while a female could not divorce at all. Some sayings of the rabbis of the day also give us interesting insights in these matters:

1. It is well for those whose children are male, but ill for those whose children are female.
2. At the birth of a boy all are joyful, but at the birth of a girl all are sad.
3. When a boy comes into the world, peace comes into the world;

when a girl comes, nothing comes.

4.   Our teachers have said: four qualities are evident in women: they are greedy at their food, eager to gossip, lazy and jealous.

This certainly does not say much for women and their place in ancient Palestine. Their condition was at best was very bleak!

A word must be said about the gospels. In light of biblical scholarship over the past two hundred years, both biblical and historical criticism, we recognize that the gospels are not simply straightforward factual reports of eyewitnesses of the events in the life of Jesus of Nazareth. They are rather four different faith statements reflecting at least four different early Christian communities who believed Jesus was the Messiah. They were composed from a variety of sources, written and oral, over a period of time in response to the needs felt in the communities and the individuals at the time. Consequently, they are multi-layered. Since these writers were not critical historians of the modern variety, they were not particularly intent in recording the actual words of Jesus himself, nor were they much concerned about weeding out their own cultural biases - perhaps they were not even aware they existed.

Our understanding of scripture today does not impugn the historical character of the gospels, it merely describes them more accurately in order that we may evaluate more accurately as well. The religious value of this technique lies in the fact that we are enabled to know with greater precision what Jesus meant by certain statements and certain acts as they were reported by the first century communities. This knowledge enables us, as well, to make vital distinctions between religious truths that are to be handed on and the time-conditioned categories and customs involved

3. Jesus - The Feminist

in expressing these truths. When the fact that no negative attitudes by Jesus toward women are portrayed in the gospels is set side by side with the recently discerned "communal faith-statement" understanding of the nature of the gospels, the importance of the former is greatly enhanced. For whatever Jesus did or said is handed on to us only through the eyes of the first Christians. If there was no very special significance in a particular custom or concept, we would not expect that concept or custom to be reflected by Jesus. The fact that the overwhelmingly negative attitude toward women in Palestine did not come through the early Christian communal understanding by itself clearly underscores the great religious importance Jesus attached to his positive attitude - his feminist attitude - toward women. The fact that women are treated as human beings is a constitutive part of the gospel, i.e. *the good news of Jesus of Nazareth*!

In the gospels there are numerous occasions on which Jesus discussed *scripture* with a woman. We should keep in mind that not only was this improper in his day, it might very well have been considered *obscene*. The decision of Jesus to challenge this existing custom was extraordinary.

Moreover, not only did Jesus have women learning from him, he also had women following him in his travels. To wit: The Gospel of Mark, chapter 15, verse 40 and following states: "He made his way through the town and villages preaching and proclaiming the Good News of the kingdom of God. With him were the Twelve, as well as certain women ... who provided out of their own resources." The significance of this can only be understood properly when we recall that not only were women *not* to read or *study scripture*, but they were not even to leave their households. To be sure, this is a radical break with custom and culture!

On yet another occasion, Jesus deliberately, it seems, violated the common code concerning the relationship of women to men. It is the familiar story of Jesus and the woman at the well, a woman from Samaria (cf. John 4:5ff.). While waiting for his disciples who were about getting food, a woman from Samaria approached the well in the village to draw water. Some items of interest are present here: (1) Jews would normally not associate with Samaritans and (2) a man would not normally speak with a woman in public, especially if the man happened to be a rabbi and finally, (3) a man, especially a teacher or rabbi, would *not* be discussing theology with a woman anywhere, let alone in public. Nevertheless, Jesus startles the woman by addressing her and initiating a conversation. The woman was aware of the peculiarity of the situation as she replied: "How is it that you, a Jew, ask a drink of me, a woman of Samaria?" Even though Samaritans were hated by Jews, it was a much more flagrant breach of code when he spoke with a woman in public. As The Gospel of John relates it in terms of the reaction of his disciples: "His disciples returned, and were surprised to find him speaking to a woman, though none of them asked, 'What do you want from her?' or 'Why are you talking to her'?" Indeed, Jesus bridged the gap of inequality even further when in his conversation with the woman he revealed himself as the Messiah. "The woman said to him I know that the Messiah is coming ... Jesus said to her, 'I who speak to you am he.'"

A final consideration: marriage! In this venue, i.e. marriage, the *relative* dignity of a woman is characteristic. In the case of Jesus, however, once again we find him taking an unpopular road and elevating woman to a place of equality with man. He argues that women have the same rights and responsibilities in marriage as men. In Jewish law it was possible for men to have more than one wife, although the reverse was not possible. Divorce was simple: the man just gave his wife a "writ of divorcement."

3. Jesus - The Feminist

The reverse, again, was not possible. Women were simply property! They were able to be collected and dismissed at will: a flagrant double standard. Jesus rejected these practices and insisted that men and women were to have the same rights and responsibilities toward each other.

Well, Well, Well, What have We Here?!

Unfortunately, unlike Jesus, the Church - and to a great degree modern society - assimilated his views in a rather rigid fashion. The church was and is very cognizant of civil and social rights but they did not, and still often do not, extend them very well into the realm of human sexuality or the realm of marriage. Over the centuries the general rule for women has been: the church, children, and the kitchen and only a minor role in the first, if at all.

We have a lot of catching up to do, if we are to be on the same playing field as Jesus of Nazareth - who espoused these views some two thousand years ago. We had better get moving.

4. Some Poetic Reflections

REMEMBERING CHRISTMAS

Music fills the air around us;
 Smiles are on the faces of people everywhere -
  Especially children - eyes bright
   With anticipation and joy!
Christmas! - a marvelous - but fleeting moment in our lives!
Overcome by the excitement, splendor and delight,
 We miss the essence of the season - "Love Incarnate!"
  A love without boundaries,
   A love of and for all people,
    A love - the font of all joy and happiness,
A love with power to bring peace in our heart,
 To give hope to a world in need,
  Peace to a world blinded by its
   Greed and emptiness!
Nevertheless, we can be joyful,
 We can be hopeful,
  We can be thankful
   For this wonderful, most gracious gift,
    The gift of "Love Incarnate,"
 Which brightens every human spirit,

Warms every human heart,

Enlightens every mind,

And strengthens every will

With its peaceful, loving,

Life-giving Presence!

LOVE INCARNATE

Once, in ages past

    Love became incarnate!

Yet, this love,

    Ever was -

        Ever is -

            Ever shall be!

So simple - yet profound,

    But they missed its coming.

So gentle, so kind,

    So universally compassionate -

        Yet, they missed its coming - then

            Just as we miss Its Presence, Now!

The world we see -

    Prances and dances -

        Rises and falls around us.

The world pronounces its power,

    Decrees its authority -

        Affirms and asserts its dominance.

But overlooks its failures and weaknesses,

    Dismisses its temporality, its finitude.

Love incarnate - genuine before its eyes -

    Goes without recognition!

This Existent

Part II - Thoughts About Jesus of Nazareth

Persistent,
>Consistent love
Simply IS! As always, as ever!
Oddly, in the strangest of places!

In the eyes,
>In the hearts - and even
>>In the wrinkles of the aged.
In the smiles,
>The chattering voices of children,
In the spirit and will of
>Those who seek,
In the city-puddle rainbows
>And the smoggy skies
>>Of darkened huddled cities,
In the simple gift of a greeting,
>A handshake,
>>An embrace for
>>>The lonely,
>>>>The poor,
>>>>>The estranged.
This Love Universal -
>This Love Incarnate -
>>Challenges and encourages us
>>To see,
>>>To feel,
>>>>To taste,
>>>>>To touch and to be touched
By the heart and hand of the Eternal,

4. Some Poetic Reflections

The divinity known not by one name only,

But by many - the One is Love Eternal!

Good News Anyone?!

Part III - Some Comments about Joseph and Mary

1. Joseph - The Forgotten Father of Jesus

The events surrounding the lives of Joseph, Mary, and Jesus are controversial, especially those pertaining to the birth of Jesus. There are a myriad of ways to examine this issue, e.g. there are those who would argue Joseph himself was the father of the child, there are others would argue that a Captain in the Roman army around this time was the father, still others would argue it was some other person, and, of course, there is the account we have in the gospel of Matthew. Cases could be made for any of these scenarios. However, let us, for argument sake, presume the traditional version.

One of the unsung heroes of the Christian faith is Joseph, the husband of Mary. The biblical accounts mentions him only in passing, and were it not for the comments in Matthew's gospel, we would know only he was a native and resident of Nazareth, the husband of Mary, and most likely died before the crucifixion of Jesus. Otherwise the record is silent. To be sure, the church has canonized him, and no scene of the nativity is complete without him. Nevertheless, our attention is usually fixed on the baby in the manger and on Mary his mother for that is where the action is. Joseph is, at best, one of those decorative and seldom studied figures who are seated or standing around the new-born child.

The arresting fact is that Joseph is there at all. He had been engaged to marry Mary, who was perhaps his cousin, and their betrothal according to religious law had the binding force of a legal marriage. And, then, Mary was found to be pregnant. The law decreed that faithlessness on the part of the woman carried the death penalty, although the future husband, should he not wish to exact the full penalty of the law, could give his promised bride a bill of divorce. It is understandable that Joseph, in love with Mary and assuming her to be in love with him, received with great distress the unsettling news that she was carrying the child of someone else. According to Rabbinic assumption, pregnancy became evident three months after conception and therefore widows and divorcees were required to wait three months after their separation from their earlier husbands before being married again. The anguish of Joseph over the disclosure that his bride-to-be was pregnant, mocking as it did their love for each other, is cloaked in the straightforward declaration that Joseph was a man of principle and would not demand any harsh penalty for Mary's breach of faith, but could under the circumstances have nothing further to do with her. He was a kindly man, unwilling to subject his finance either to death or to public disgrace; but he was also a righteous man, unable now to accept her as his wife. He could not have known she was "with child by the Holy Spirit." Mary was prepared to accept the announcement that she, an unmarried young woman, would conceive and bear a son. Miracles are self-authenticating for those who accept them; and no force of persuasion will make them credible to the unbelieving. Talmudic law defines a Jew as the child of a Jewish mother, because that is the sure side. Joseph knew that the child of Mary would not be his.

Joseph's decision to send Mary away did not come easily. He made no impetuous move. He considered the matter carefully, thoughtfully, and with heavy heart; and as so often happens to people under stress, he dreamed about it. Dreams, although we may not even yet understand them, have played a part in the life of humankind. In the days of Jesus the rabbis were divided about the value that should be attributed to dreams. Some considered them to have no value at all, while others thought them to be a weak form of prophecy. Among the latter group some thought that, just as there was true and false prophecy, so there could be true and false dreams. Some rabbis declared everything depended on an accurate interpretation of the dream; dreams not interpreted, they argued are like unread letters. But interpreted dreams would be fulfilled to the way in which they were interpreted. It seems evident that the interpretation of dreams was neither definitive nor helpful.

God Works in Mysterious Ways

Whatever we may think of all this, the story tells us Joseph appre-

1. Joseph - The Forgotten Father of Jesus

hended in a dream the message that would become decisive for his life. "Joseph, son of David," it went, "do not be afraid to take Mary home with you as your wife. It is by the Holy Spirit that she has conceived this child. She will bear a son; and you shall give him the name Jesus, for he will save his people from their sins." To understand the importance attached to names, we must realize that the bible records only six persons to whom God gave names before they were born: Isaac (Genesis 17:19), his half-brother Ishmael (Genesis 16:11), the kings Solomon (I Chronicles 22:9) and Josiah (I Kings 13:2), John the Baptist (Luke 1:13) and Jesus (Matthew 1: 21). Joseph was to take Mary, accept her child, and name him. The name Jesus is an abbreviated form of the Hebrew Joshua, which means "Yahweh (God) is salvation." The name came to Joseph as a revelation, for rabbinic speculation about the name of the Messiah had long been rife and inconclusive. Already we begin to sense something of the knowledge Joseph had of his people's history, of his faith in God's promise to redeem his people, and of his willingness to take his small part in the fulfillment of that promise. The heartbreaking news of Mary's pregnancy was, in spite of Joseph's anger and hurt and possible legal recourse, becoming an unlikely announcement of hope and joy.

"When Joseph woke from sleep, he did as the angel of the Lord had commanded him; he took Mary home to be his wife." In these decisive words the righteousness of Joseph emerges; he awoke form his dreaming and married Mary. With that act of faith and commitment he set the course of his life. Not that it made all that much difference to anyone else. Mary would have borne her child, who no doubt would have accomplished his work without being brought up by Mary and Joseph. But speculation of this kind is fruitless, for Joseph and not someone else became Jesus' father; and Jesus became Joseph's son, not the son of some-

Part III - Some Comments about Joseph and Mary

one else. Who can attach proper significance to all the contingencies of history? Joseph's obedience to the command that he be courageous and marry Mary, despite his better judgment, is the focus of our attention. And what do we see?

First: though his final decision was against his religious upbringing and moral sensibility, Joseph's love for Mary was stronger than his fear of what people would think when her child arrived early, or even than whatever he may have thought about what she had or had not done. He became persuaded that his own honor, legal tradition, and public opinion that might be leveled against him for trying by marriage to rescue a woman from disgrace were not decisive characteristics for apprehending God's will. Public morality and legal tradition would have supported and applauded his decision to put Mary away; but Joseph had learned, however feebly and inchoately, that God works in mysterious ways that truth is stranger than fiction, if you like; that love cannot be measured, though it may be tested, by honor or public opinion or legal regulation. In the story, the angel did not tell Joseph to marry Mary, but rather that he should not fear to take her as his wife if he indeed loved her; for God, not evil, was at work in her life.

How could Joseph be sure of that? He could not be sure, then or ever. And that leap of faith is the first mark of his righteousness. All life is like that. Research and prudence, law and tradition, desire and courage play their necessary roles in helping us decide what to do. But in the end we fly by the seat of our own pants, hoping that our planning has been intelligent, our desires noble, and our faith true. Probabilities give us some hope and stamina, but certainty comes from faith. We must decide if we have heard God's word for our lives correctly and on that decision we stake our lives. Joseph's faith that God had spoken to him in and through this anguish of his life, and his decision to act on that word are the first marks of his righteousness.

Far more is at stake here than Joseph's love and concern for Mary, important and critical as that was. He was told to name this child and to name the child was to accept the child as his own. Moreover, he was told to name the child, Jesus, i.e. Savior, and in so doing he accepted God's promise of redemption as being fulfilled in this child. All the longing of Israel for redemption found expression and fulfillment in that name. Who among us would dare predict the future significance of any of our infant children? It is difficult enough to make some statement about the likelihood for our university graduates to make significant contributions to the nation or the world. But here Joseph is asked to name Mary's child, Jesus, in the full expectation that Jesus would save his people from their sins. Whether or not Joseph really had such grand hopes for the boy we are unable to really say; but he did call him Jesus and took pains to see that he escape King Herod's slaughter of children two years old and under, and that he have a proper education in the synagogue.

The promises about God's salvation of the people obviously meant something to Joseph otherwise the angel's word to him would have signified nothing. Joseph was living in expectation that God would reveal God's self in power and mercy, making the glory of God known to a surprised and longing world. Joseph may even have had some notions about how that revelation would occur, but he was willing to abandon his own ideas in the expectation of Mary's child of promise. His marriage to Mary carried with it his own hope for the redemption of his people. What a conception of marriage! What a hope to treasure, nourish and live by!

Part III - Some Comments about Joseph and Mary

Most of us are not so optimistic. Our visions for the world are tamed by expediency or weariness or hopelessness - especially in recent times. Tomorrow we fear is unlikely to be better than today, more likely to be worse. Our children will be lucky to have lives as good as ours; so we hang on in grim desperation. Joseph had no grand illusions either. Nothing in the scripture suggests that he ever spoke about his reasons for marrying Mary or for bringing up her child. But he did have hope; hope that carried him beyond the heartache and foreboding of his engagement to Mary to the coming deliverance of Israel. Joseph had an essential and lively vision for the future and that is the second mark of his righteousness.

Finally, we read of Joseph that "he took Mary home to be his wife, but had no intercourse with her until her son was born. And he named the child Jesus." That long wait until the child was born must be seen as a third mark of Joseph's righteousness. However he may have understood or intended his behavior, Joseph was living out the consequences of taking the pregnant Mary home to be his wife. He accepted in faithfulness and patience the obligations, as he perceived them, of his decision to be her husband. Everything we read about him, little as it is, reinforces the perception that Joseph was a prudent husband and father, looking out intelligently and vigilantly for the safety and welfare of Mary and Jesus. What we may infer here is the daily routine of a diligent and devoted spouse, who in fidelity to his marriage commitment does not look backward or pretend to be more or less than he is. He gives love and hope a chance by his steadfast commitment to his promise. We have here the long walk of the believer - humbly and willingly obedient - till the time be fulfilled. And when the child is born, Joseph names him Jesus!

1. Joseph - The Forgotten Father of Jesus

Perhaps Joseph's righteousness is less spectacular than the faithful submission of Mary, but it is nevertheless moving in its simple fidelity. Joseph reveals the life of faith, from the moment of his encounter with anxiety, through the difficult hours of his decision, and on into the protracted patience and restraint of living with his choice. What he knew of the outcome of his venture was only a wild surmise. He did not live to see his son's last days, and even if he had, his faith would still have been severely tested. He believed, and God reckoned that to him as righteousness!

2. Mary, the Mother of Jesus of Nazareth

It may be somewhat surprising that a Protestant theologian, such as myself, would be reflecting on Mary, the Mother of Jesus of Nazareth. After all, is not Mary the province of our Roman Catholic brothers and sisters? And do we not disagree with some, if not most, of their dogma concerning the young Jewish mother of Jesus? She is seen, especially in popular Roman Catholic piety, as almost being a *co-redeemer*, as a mediator along with Jesus of Nazareth, between humanity and God. Even one of the most influential Protestant theologians of the 20th Century, Paul Tillich, states in his *Systematic Theology*, Volume I, page 128: "…the Virgin Mother Mary reveals 'nothing' to Protestants." This is a view, I submit, which is held commonly among most Protestant Christians regardless of their denomination.

However, to take this position is, perhaps, to miss a major contribution to our Christian faith. Certainly, we Protestants pay simple homage to her during Christmastide; we acknowledge her passing role in the great creeds of the early church, e.g. The Nicene Creed (325 C.E.), The Niceno-Constantinopolitan Creed (381 C.E.) and The Definition of Chalcedon

(451 C.E.). At the same time, we do not acknowledge or examine the inner qualities of this young Jewish woman who was the mother of Jesus of Nazareth. Why is this so? Let me say this: it is, in my view, primarily due to the magnification, the glorification, the *almost deification* of Mary by the pious among us, especially those in the Roman Catholic tradition. This attitude toward her became inevitable when during the early to middle age centuries of our Christian history, Jesus the Christ became remote, as far removed from human experience as God, the Father. I remember a colleague of mine in the department of theology of the University of Dayton, a Roman Catholic Sister, in the Order of the Sisters of St. Joseph, pointing out that God seemed so remote, so powerful and vengeful, that ordinary people turned away in fear; this eventually became true of Jesus of Nazareth as well. With both God, the Father, and Jesus so powerful, so distant, people appealed to Jesus through his mother, Mary. And, the rest is history, so to speak.

As a young theologian and a junior faculty member at the University of Dayton, I was invited to attend the inaugural lecture of The Rev. Theodore Koehler, S.M., who was to become the Curator of the University's world-renown Marian Library and Director of the Institute for Mariological Studies. I was invited, in part, because of my generally liberal views. At the time, as a liberal Protestant, I really had no interest in Mariology; I was in total accord with Paul Tillich on this matter. Nevertheless, I ultimately made the decision to attend the lecture. A trusted colleague advised me that Father Koehler's presentation would be significantly different from any I had ever heard on the subject and not at all similar to the one I held at the time of Jesus' mother, Mary.

I was not deceived, Father Koehler's view did indeed present a very

2. Mary, the Mother of Jesus of Nazareth

different view of Mary. Certainly, as a Roman Catholic, as a priest, and as one of the world's leading Mariologists, his view was, in part, traditional, but with a marked difference. Father Koehler presented Mary as a very *human* figure, as a person who had a deep faith commitment to her God, as one who demonstrated positive human virtues, such as: loyalty, compassion, strength, and most importantly - love! His view was neither offensive to me as a Protestant, nor was it dogmatic, as I had previously experienced. It was highly metaphorical; steeped in the richness of symbolic language and, as such, very appealing.

Parenting the Son of God

If you search the scriptures, Koehler's understanding of Mary is very evident, particularly in her dealings with the uniqueness of her son as he confounded the rabbis and teachers of all sorts. If you examine the manner in which she handled Jesus' own rejection of *her* when she went to him in a time of need and his response to her was very direct: "who is my mother?" or perhaps, most significantly at the crucifixion of her son, Jesus, where we find her "standing firmly at the cross," not weeping nor wailing; she manifests powerful, strong characteristics of what it means to be truly and fully human, what it means to have a faith commitment that is real and deep, what it is to deal directly with joy, pain, rejection, suffering and love at their deepest levels. Mary may not be the "Queen of Heaven;" she may not be a "co-Redeemer" with Jesus the Christ, but she is a very real, very powerful, moving paradigm of what it means to possess those qualities which make us to be the kind of person(s) our God, the God of Jesus of Nazareth and the God of Mary, as well the God of you and me, desires us to be.

That was an enlightening evening for me. It gave me new insights not only into Mary, the Mother of Jesus of Nazareth, but allowed me to use her as a paradigm, along with her son, Jesus of Nazareth, for what it truly means to be human, to be a child of God, to have been created imago Dei, i.e. in God's very image.

It was an enriching experience to say the very least!

3. Mary: Humble Beginnings - Powerful Ending

Although I did not grow up with great admiration or much concern for, or about, Mary, the Mother of Jesus, in my more mature years

I have come to appreciate her more. Perhaps you have as well. Mary is given the most astonishing task of carrying God's essence, that is: God's love, into the world. You may recall one of the titles given to her by the ancient church and used so frequently by our Roman Catholic friends is: "*Theotokos*: the God-bearer." And what is even more amazing is the fact that she said "Yes" this enormous task and challenge. Remember, Mary was just a very *young girl* at the time. *Almah* in the Hebrew, meaning a young woman of marriageable age, or more simply, a *young person*, is the term used by the prophet Isaiah to designate this in the text (Isaiah 7:14) "…behold a virgin shall conceive and bear a son, and shall call his name Immanuel." The Septuagint (a Greek translation of the Hebrew text) translates this Hebrew term using the Greek word *parthenos* or "virgin" whereas the more appropriate term in this context is *neanis*, meaning a young person, and is found in most other Greek translations of this very well-known Hebrew text.

Let me suggest that the church, that is to say: the Christian community is also a type of *Theotokos* (God-bearer) to the world. This motif is especially clear in the season of beginnings, the season of new creation, redemption, and grace whereby we are inspired to bring God into a world in great need by sharing warm meals, warm coats, smiles and gifts of all varieties for those around us and around the world - all of which is a very appropriate way to honor a child whose family had no place to stay - a child in whom the fullness of God's love and grace are manifest, namely, the incarnation of the very *love of God*.

Moreover, *we* are also *Theotokoi* (God-bearers) as we preach - in a variety of ways, sometimes even silent ways - teach, and sing words of hope and promise to people who rarely hear either, or when and as we offer a hearty, "Come in!" to those who doubt their welcome - the outcasts, the fringe members of our societies, those who are scorned by the powerful, by the elite, by the so-called "important, influential people" in life. And as we do these things in and through faith and its expression in concrete acts of gentleness and kindness throughout our lives, we make clear the presence of God and God's love, compassion, mercy, power and grace visible and available to all.

Say What?!

In a world of filled with negativity, full of hate, with its pursuit of wealth and power, in a world filled with anxiety and emptiness in the lives of so many people, the "Yes" of this simple young Jewish girl, Mary, to God's invitation is a model of exquisite humanness. The hope she

3. Mary: Humble Beginnings - Powerful Ending

reflects, the hope you and I now possess in Jesus of Nazareth, the One we call the Christ, allows us to say "Yes" to invitations to serve and to say "Yes" to new ideas when logic would clearly dictate a resounding "No!" Truly this is the baffling challenge of the gospel to each and every one of us just as it was to Mary.

The novelist and Presbyterian minister-theologian, Frederick Buechner, in his work *Peculiar Treasures* (page 39), describes this posture most poignantly and most beautifully in these words:

> "She [Mary] struck the angel Gabriel as hardly old enough to have a child at all, let alone this child, but he'd been entrusted with a message to give her and he gave it.
>
> He told her what the child was to be named, and who he was to be, and Something about the mystery that was to come upon her. 'You mustn't Be afraid, Mary.' He said.
>
> As he said it, he only hoped she wouldn't notice that beneath the great golden wings he himself was trembling with fear to think that the whole future of creation now hung upon the answer of a young girl."

In his little narrative here Buechner has given us an insight into the great importance of this specific event and how powerful and important our responses are - even if we do not totally understand their significance at the moment. And I must say - in astonished agreement - how grateful I am for all the *Yes-sayers* who have responded over the centuries to the call and challenge of our God of Love, Peace, and Grace. I continue to pray the hope and joy, the peace and love of this eternal message of Incarnate Love may be, and may continue to be, real in the world in which we live today, a world so desperately in search of and in need of such a message.

Part III - Some Comments about Joseph and Mary

Thus, I say to you, Mary says to you, and all those who have responded over these past two millennia say to you: as always, *Pax et Caritas tecum!* "Peace and Love (be) with you!"

John 3:16

3. Mary: Humble Beginnings - Powerful Ending

Part IV - The Redemptive Work of Jesus of Nazareth

1. Prologue to Jesus' Seven Last Words from the Cross

We are so familiar with the term "Good Friday" that its use in the context of death and suffering of an innocent man never disturbs or puzzles us, primarily because we never really think about it. It has become too familiar. Certainly anyone who knew nothing at all of the facts of the Christian faith, or had no previous acquaintance with its meaning, if that person heard the story told here in regard to *this* Friday, would wonder why anyone would choose to call it *good*. It is strange, is it not, to take a day on which an innocent man was brutally murdered, a day in which the power of justice was turned on its proverbial head, a day when the forces of religion even with all their seemingly good intentions, appears to have been blind and labeled it for all time:, "Good" Friday! But what is so good about physical pain and agony? What is so good about innocent suffering and an unmerited death? Nothing! Absolutely nothing!

So then, why or how is it possible for us call this Friday Good?

Not for any sentimental or romantic reason, to be sure! Perhaps it is because of the glorious and magnificent demonstration of the love of God that is contained in this event in the life of Jesus. I believe the Apostle Paul succinctly captured this idea in his letter to the Romans when he wrote: "Where sin abounded, grace abounded much more!" Permit me to para-phrase Paul's comment in this manner: *Where evil and hatred abounds, the love and grace of God, is stronger, more abundant, and, just as light dispels darkness, the love of God dispels evil and hatred.* This is not simply a casual observation of this Jesus-event, it is an entirely new *world-view*, a richer, fuller way in which to live. These few words of the great apostle simply state for us that the greatest power we can ever experience in life is the love of God.

There are many skeptics who will say: Can that really be true? Can anyone really believe it, be certain of it, or live by it? The response of the Christian faith is that it was made true on a hill called Golgotha, on this Friday ... and that is why we call it "Good!"

Not So Good Friday

1. Prologue to Jesus' Seven Last Words from the Cross

No one who has examined this scene will deny that evil was present manifesting its grossness, its ugliness and vulgarity. The interesting fact, however, is that this evil was not perpetrated by thugs, hoodlums, or muggers, or the dregs of society, but rather by refinement and decency. No, Jesus fell into the hands of society's most respected citizens: the politely washed hands of religious leaders, lawyers, political leaders and, intellectuals. If it had been otherwise, it would still have been evil, but at least, somewhat more understandable. At the cross of Jesus, evil abounded subtly, not wearing the lurid colors of low crime and dark passion, but a somber, sinister scheme painted in respectable shades of rationality, decency and order.

Did the love of God abound more? Did the love of God assure mastery of even that monstrous situation? It would be easy—and even understandable - for us to turn away from this heart-rending scene and say, "No, evil has won! Jesus, after all, died! No one was there to help, no one to deliver, no one to save him!"

There are tragedies more important than the tragedy of death. There are more important victories than the victory of being delivered. Did the faith of Jesus fail him? No! Did his love become cold and bitter? No! Did he lose spirit? No? Did his vision fail or his hope perish? No! So, where evil seemed to be victorious, God's love was much more abundant, much more powerful! Indeed, everything that matters to a person in his or her life - however troublesome or difficult, the love of God is more powerful, more abundant, and stronger than human brutality !

Perhaps we can sum up our thoughts in this manner: this man Jesus of Nazareth, this cross, and our God have the power to make not only all our *Fridays* good, but *all* our days. This particular Friday, the one we set aside, is not just one dark spot in human history being redeemed and set aglow, but God is always seen to be a redeeming love which can make all our difficulties, trials, and sufferings events filled with meaning, strength and love. The love of God is always greater than our worst difficulties, always greater than our deepest need. We can always take our problems, our sorrows, our temptations, our failures, all the things in life that get us down, put them on the scale and the cross of Jesus of Nazareth, who is, the very incarnation of God's Love and they all will always be outweighed!

1st Word from the Cross

Text: Luke 23: 32-34: "Two criminals were also led out with him for execution, and when they came to the place called 'The Skull' (Golgotha), they crucified him with the criminals, one on each side of him. But Jesus was himself was saying: "Father, forgive them; they do not know what they are doing."

With Jesus of Nazareth hanging on the cross his teaching is no longer simply *theory*, it becomes *reality*! When we read the Sermon on the Mount, Jesus commands us to love our enemies; here on the cross Jesus himself obeys this command. In the Sermon on the Mount Jesus of Nazareth tells us to do good to those who oppose us and who use us spitefully; here on the cross he follows his own teaching. In the Sermon on the Mount, Jesus of Nazareth advises us the hallmark of discipleship is forgiveness. Here on the cross he gives us a concrete illustration of that central teaching.

I have often felt if I had any reservations, any doubts about God's love being incarnated in Jesus of Nazareth, this would be the place these reservations and doubts would be resolved. Here, in this event, it seems so clear that the love of God and God's own humanity is evident. It is not too difficult to understand why one may have difficulty with such teachings as the *Virgin Birth*, or be unconvinced by his so-called *miracles* and remain unconvinced of God's presence in his life. But, and this is a very significant *but*, it is very hard to understand how anyone could go to the foot of the cross, hear these words of *forgiveness* and not join with the Roman captain in charge of the crucifixion and say: "Truly, truly, this man was the Son of God."

When I read, understand, and appropriate these words in the context of exquisite agony of the spirit and the excruciating pain inflicted on the body, I believe I am hearing something unequivocally human, but, at the same time, something demanding much more for these words so far transcend the bounds of ordinary love and forgiveness and kindness - they demand the fullness of the presence of God in his human being - Jesus of Nazareth. That Jesus could speak this word of forgiveness gives us confidence and heartens us in our understanding that the kind of God proclaimed in the Christian gospel is a God who even in the torment of death by crucifixion could say: "Forgive!"

The more I think about it, the more I am convinced this gracious word is a type of *creed*, concise, succinct, but tremendous in what it comprehends! In this brief statement we discover the Christian understanding of God and the Christian understanding of humanness. Let us look at what it does say - about humanity, about we, finite human beings which will allow us, to see in sharper outline and in greater detail, what this word has to say about God.

Part IV - The Redemptive Work of Jesus of Nazareth

"They do not know what they are doing!" To whom was Jesus referring? Was he simply asking forgiveness for the soldiers who were simply doing their duty and had to carry out this bloody execution by crucifixion? Is the forgiveness here that limited? Did it not also include the priests? The scribes? The Pharisees who, in their treacherous, jealous plotting produced this horrible event? Or, does it not include *all of us* so that even we today thousands of miles and years removed from the event are included with Jesus still praying, "Father, forgive them for they do not know what they are doing?"

What a revelation is in those words: "They do not know what they are doing!" Some have argued sin is simply ignorance, that is: the reason people do wrong is they do not know or understand what is right. Teach them to do right and the problem is solved says the ancient philosopher, along with many others. What fallacy? What a rationalization! Certainly, sometimes we do not know, but more often than not, we, with perfect intellectual understanding of what we *ought* to do or not do, beg off our responsibility saying: "I didn't know."

So then, was Jesus mistaken when he said: "They do not know what they are doing?" Maybe the soldiers, maybe, but the priests, the Pharisees, the teachers of the law, all of us today - whom he is certainly ready to forgive - can we say did what was done in ignorance? If we are honest with ourselves, it is hard to believe so.

Yet, Jesus was not wrong either. There is intellectual ignorance which makes mistakes for the lack of information. This is easily remedied. But, Jesus is not speaking about this type of ignorance. There is a deeper

1st Word from the Cross

ignorance of spirit which arises not from the lack of information, but the lack of direction, attitude and inner motive. From this we all suffer. In the deepest and most tragic sense of the word, "we do not know what we are doing."

In our innermost being we often do not know who or what we are, namely, God's children, or to whom we ultimately belong and therefore inevitably do not really know what we are doing.

It is so easy for us to think we are the center of reality, the axis upon which the universe revolves so that without meaning to be vain, proud or demanding we expect life to meet us on our terms. And because we *are* so important, we can do the most crude, most cruel things conceivable to gain our ends. We can always justify ourselves in our conduct, what we would quickly condemn in others.

Every Lenten season we heap reproach on the Jewish priesthood for what it did to Jesus of Nazareth, the Christ. Yet, if we had been able to interview Annas or Caiaphas the day after that fateful Good Friday, either one of them would have been able to give us a perfectly reasonable explanation regarding his conduct and one in which he himself most sincerely believed. Furthermore had we been in those priestly robes, it is highly likely we would have done the same things with much the same conviction that what we were doing was clearly correct. We do not know what we do because we are forgetful of who we are and generally we crucify,- metaphorically speaking, those who try to tell us. Is this not precisely what happened to Jesus of Nazareth?

There is, however, another aspect to consider in this sentence. It is the most important affirmation: "Father, forgive them!" If ignorance and unacknowledged, unrepentant self-centeredness is Jesus' verdict on human nature, here is his final belief about God. "Father, forgive them." These two phrases go together, do they not? It is because God is loving as a father would be toward his child, that God's nature is also forgiving. This forgiveness is the most basic, fundamental experience that we humans can have with God. We see God as Father, not because in some vague way we see God as Creator, as the One who endowed us with life, but rather because when we return from our wanderings, we find God waiting for us with open arms and a welcoming heart. But how do we find the courage to come, or the nerve, if you will? We come to God and ask for forgiveness because we have been persuaded and convinced the "heart of the Eternal" is the "heart of a gracious Father." We have seen it here in the cross.

In these words from the cross is the answer to so many of our human searching including the brutal truth about ourselves and the gracious truth about our God. If we see only the brutal truth about human nature which is so abundant in our life experiences, we can easily become cynical and despairing. If we see *only* the gracious and glorious truth about our God, we easily fall into a false optimism and a light responsibility. However, if we see both, even partially, the full extent of our darkness mastered by a fuller, richer love of God, we can hang on the Cross, and our crosses today, and keep a strong faith.

Whenever I think of these things, I always remember the prayer Dietrich Bonhoeffer offered for himself and his fellow prisoners as they were being led to execution at the Flossenburg Concentration Camp in April of 1945. His fellow prisoners requested him to pray.

1st Word from the Cross

"In the dawn of the day I call to Thee

Help me pray

Direct my thoughts to Thee

I cannot manage on my own

It is dark within me, but there is light in Thee

I am lonely, but Thou will not leave me

I am faint of heart, but know Thou will help me

I am troubled, but know that in Thee is peace

I am bitter, but in Thee is endurance

I do not understand Thy ways

But Thou understandeth them for me."

2nd Word from the Cross

Text: Luke 23: 39-43 - One of the criminals hanging there covered him with abuse, and said: "Aren't you the Christ? Why don't you save yourself - and us?" But the other criminal responded and said: "Aren't you afraid of God even when you are getting the same punishment as he is? And it's fair enough for us, for we've only got what we deserve, but this man never did anything wrong in his life." Then he said: "Jesus, remember me when you come into your kingdom." And Jesus answered and said: "I tell you truly, this very day you will be with me in paradise."

Hardly any character in the entire Christian scripture has been the subject of more speculation or romancing than this repentant thief who hung beside Jesus of Nazareth in death. Actually, all we know of him is contained in this single passage found only in the Gospel of Luke. Nevertheless pious legend has given him a name, Dismas, and pious speculation seeking to discover and understand this eleventh hour change has created whole biographies of him.

The fact remains, however, whoever or whatever he was, as far as history is concerned, he appears on the scene only in this one unforgettable moment. Was he a political revolutionary or an assassin? No one really knows! Could he have been, along with his companion in crucifixion, an associate of the celebrated rebel, Barabbas who had been released that morning at the behest of the angry mob?

I will not pretend to know what suddenly prompted a change of heart of this man whose life with as most likely dedicated to violence and murder and who, perhaps, had never so much as seen Jesus of Nazareth until this fateful day when they were led out to die together. Perhaps he heard that word of Jesus: "Father forgive them for they do not know what they are doing." Perhaps the pain and cursing of this moment had started him wondering and thinking. And then out of the darkness of Golgotha the next voice we hear in an unforgettable request is: "Lord, remember me when you come into your kingdom." The general understanding of Jesus' reply is that it is never too late to turn to him in faith and repentance for here is a man, we may say with reasonable certainty, whose entire life had been Godless and evil. In the final hours of his life, a life lived in hell, he enters paradise with a single change of heart. Down to the end, down to the very last breath, this is a possibility open to all. If this word means anything at all, it means with Jesus of Nazareth, God's incarnate *Love* there is never a *too late*.

2nd Word from the Cross

This is the obvious meaning of this text. And if we spend no more time with it, it is for that reason: it *is obvious*! There are other things to consider.

First here is a magnificent example of the way in which God's greatness and love exceeds all our expectations. After all, the penitent thief had only asked to be remembered. "Remember me," he said. He asked for nothing else. Unlike some of Jesus' own disciples, he did not seek any "special place of honor." He did not even ask to be let off from any penalty he might have to pay for his life of crime and evil.

Nor was he seeking to evade any form of justice he would be assigned in the world to come. He simply asked not to be forgotten. He made that request to a man he was now convinced would be the Lord of that next world.

The request was modest. However, look at the response. "This very day you will be with me in paradise." Not I will remember you, but a response far more than anyone could ever have imagined. Not I'll remember you when I come into my kingdom, but "today!" You will not have to wait; it will not be postponed to some future time, but it will be "today." Not only will I remember you, I will take you with me - "today!" It will not be some vague, uncertain spot; it will be paradise. The problem for us today is not that Jesus will forget us, but rather, we have forgotten him! And there is much evidence for this in the manner in which so many of us act and live.

In this matter of asking and receiving there is another factor which for the want of a better name we shall simply call "the time-factor." Not only do we underestimate the gifts of God, we put them off into some distant future. For example: when the Apostle Paul speaks of death being swallowed up in victory, we think only of the final resurrection - eons away. When we think of, or read of, eternal life in the gospel, we think of when we die.

It is amazing how we have converted the Christian faith and message into something that only has relevance for the far distant future and an uncertain future at that. The crucified thief though much as we do: "Remember me when you come into your kingdom." And there is no telling when or if that will ever be. Not unreasonable, if for no other reason than crucified daydreamers do not become kings with kingdoms overnight.

Look again at the reply: "Today you will be with me in paradise." A future hope and possibility becomes a present reality. Some will say, true, but what else could it be, they both were going to die that very day so it would have to be *that* day.

This, however, misses the point entirely. Even if Jesus and the thief had decades yet to live, the response at this moment would have been exactly the same for these words do not so much mean to refer to the *place* they are going by virtue of their common faith, but to the new relationship into which they had entered by reason of faith. To be with Jesus in paradise is not a promise for the future; it is a possibility for the present. To be *with Jesus of Nazareth, God's love incarnate*, is to be in paradise. Undoubtedly it is an experience that will continue to be perfected as we continue to grow in faith. Heaven, or paradise so-called, is not a realm totally distinct from this world in which we live, it is an experience which

2nd Word from the Cross

interpenetrates the experiences of our humanity, our mortality. The thief did not begin his experience of paradise upon drawing his last breath in this world. He began his experience the very moment he recognized God's love incarnate in the man by his side.

Should anyone think we are dealing here in fantasy, and there will be those who so think, let me simply say that, by this, even in this world so filled with evil, contradiction and confusion, it is possible to go through one hellish situation after another, that it is possible to endure physical pain and suffering, while our hearts and spirits remain filled with peace, calm and joy. This is what we mean when we say we are in paradise while yet a part of this earthly scene of evil, change, and chance. Those who live in faith and hope, while waiting for the final triumph of God's grace, live even more in the present experience of what God's grace and love in their lives here and now.

So it was for that unknown thief on the cross; so it is even for us, today.

3rd Word from the Cross

Text: John 19: 17-27. There is something very appealing and human about this third word from the cross. Perhaps it does not blind us with the brilliance of its glory like the previous word; perhaps it does not shake us to the very depths of our being like the searching cry which will follow, nevertheless, in its human tenderness, it has a unique quality all its own.

Sometime after his conversation with the penitent thief, Jesus looked down from his cross and saw his mother standing at his feet in the company of several other women and the disciple whom he loved. It is important to underscore the fact that John states Mary was *standing* at the foot of the cross. She was not swooning or carrying on, indulging herself in some emotional display, but standing in all the pride of motherhood, with a sorrow that was too deep for tears.

We can only guess what was running through her mind. Was this the time when she remembered the word spoken to her long ago in the temple when the aged Simeon had predicted the day would come when the sword would pierce her heart also? Was this the time when she felt that stabbing pain in her soul yet knew a peace beyond the pain because she *believed* that even this awful hour had its place in God's purpose?

We can only surmise what she felt as she saw her son hanging in death. But we know what he felt when he saw his mother standing loyally by his cross. She must have been a widow by this time for there is no mention of Joseph anywhere in the story. And when the father of the family was gone, it became the duty of the eldest son to provide for his mother or, if he was unable to do it, to see that she was taken care of.

It was this filial duty that Jesus now performed, commanding his mother to the care and responsibility of John, his beloved disciple. You may well ask why he did not give the responsibility to those to whom it belonged, to his younger brothers and sisters. But the very fact they were not there at the end should be a sufficient answer to that question. Whether it was fear or shame or their dislike of him that kept them away, they had absented themselves from Calvary and so had forfeited their right and responsibility to another.

3rd Word from the Cross

I do not think it unfair for us to say Jesus had been a strange child and that Mary had not always found her motherhood easy. Back when he was twelve, he had begun to show his independence. He had run away without telling anyone. What may have occurred between that and his thirtieth birthday we are unable to say. But then when Mary was probably already a widow, badly in need of financial help, with a home to maintain, mouths to feed, children to clothe, her eldest son whose duty it ought to have been to provide had left her. I am sure she was some awareness that he had another work to do, and I am sure he did not leave without some financial provision, but it was hard sledding all the same. And the resentment of his younger brothers who had to take their place in the carpenter's shop at an early age had not made it easier.

Nor did the growing resentment and rejection help her position. At first, when Jesus had swept everything before him in a tide of popular acclaim, she had been glad to give him up and bask a little in his reflected glory. But as his support gradually fell away, as the opposition in Jerusalem gathered strength, as reports came back to her in Nazareth of the strange things he was saying and doing, she found it harder and harder to accept the situation, until finally she resolved to bring him back home to Nazareth. Probably he was fatigued, overworked; probably what he needed was rest, good food, and a mother's care.

And so she went one day with her family to ask him to come home, standing eagerly outside the door of the house where he was speaking. Then came the incredible message. He would not see them; she was not his mother; they were not his brothers; he had a new family and no longer needed them.

No, being the mother of Jesus had not been easy. And now there at the cross the worst she had feared finally came to pass. And yet, there she is by the side of her dying son! She might have said, "He made his own bed; let him lie in it." She might have said, "Last year when I tried to get him to come home, he didn't know who his mother was; I don't know how my son is." She might have done as apparently her other children had done, and gone home to hide herself for shame at having a criminal in the family. She might have - but she did not!

Many waters cannot quench love, neither can floods drown it. We may not believe Mary is the "queen of heaven," but we dare not forget Mary is a superb example of the power of human loyalty and strength of human love. Indeed, these two figures at the foot of the cross, are unforgettable pictures of what our human relationships ought to be: John, the friend who stands by to the end and whose friendship is deeper than chance or change, whose loyalty lasts; and Mary, the mother whose love will allow no misunderstanding, no imagined or real neglect, no false pride or shame to keep her from the place where she belongs.

I understand that many times our friendship is not like this, that it has a way of disappearing when things get difficult. It is so easy to grow cynical about friendship when it can vanish so quickly. You see it here at the cross. The three associates of Jesus in his earthly ministry were Peter, James and John. And now in the hour of crisis Peter was gone, James was gone, but John was there, almost as if to show us what human friendship so often is, and yet what it can - and should - be!

I also know that many times our family life is not like this. We all know how twisted and bitter family life can become, how easily close

3rd Word from the Cross

intimacy can become blazing hatred. Well, we see this here at Calvary as well. His brothers and sisters were not there. They were home crying in their pillows for the shame he had brought upon them, home nursing their resentment against that crucified fool to whom unfortunately they were related. But his mother was there, again almost as if to show us what family love so often is and yet what it can be.

Let us turn now from these two figures to the central figure on the cross. For if in Mary and John we catch the meaning of human loyalty and human love, in Jesus we see the meaning of divine love and divine loyalty, and it is unforgettable.

Is the word of Jesus not somewhat surprising? What would you expect someone to say under these circumstances? "Look, John, this is no place for my mother. Take her home with you and get her away from this." That would be very human and very understandable, a perfectly natural wish to spare her from further suffering. "Mother, this is not as bad as it seems. Dry your tears and remember that we shall meet again in a better world." That too would be perfectly natural, a desire to comfort and console.

But the surprising thing is that the first thought of Jesus for his mother is neither for her protection or consolation, but for her sheer financial well-being and economic security. On the cross itself, bearing the sin of the world, about to stare down the bottomless abyss of divine desertion, Jesus of Nazareth remembers first of all the physical and economic well-being of his mother.

There is no more dramatic an illustration of a truth we are always tending to forget. Indeed, it is a persistent heresy on the part of many people of faith that if only you can extract a person's soul from the rest of him/her, you can minister to it as a little entity all by itself. Well Jesus of Nazareth never thought that way, not even in the stress of pain and of dying. He was always aware of the primary and essential wants of the whole being, the entire personality. And surely God's concern is no less.

It is a terrible thing when your religion is so elevated that it is above the ordinary needs of human life. Yet that is precisely the fate which has overtaken the religion of so many of us. Our religion is on a Sunday level while we live on a Monday through Saturday level. So often we hear the complaint that the Christian faith and Christianity is impractical and idealistic, with nothing to say to the ordinary needs and common problems of everyday living. But I argue those who make this complaint most often believe in a God so far away and so removed from this mortal scene that God nowhere touches the problems and needs of everyday living.

All we can say is if we worship a God to whom we would never think of turning over the routine concerns and ordinary affairs that make up ninety percent of our living, we are not worshipping the God of Jesus of Nazareth, but some idol of our own design. So many of us are familiar with the God of the *crisis*, but we have never encountered the *God of the commonplace*. Our God is there to deal with birth, sickness, death, and disaster. But we should never dream of disturbing God with matters of household finance, family relationships, job difficulties, or similar problems. Our religion is just too elevated for real life.

Yet is it not true that we shall find God in the crisis only when we have effectively made an acquaintance in the commonplace? And is it not true that the God of the gospel wants to permeate all our living, no matter how commonplace, how trivial, with a sense of presence? Whenever we are tempted to believe there are aspects of our living too ordinary for God, too routine to be of concern to God, we can remember this third word from the cross.

It is a precious insight into the heart of God. The trivial necessities, the commonplace routines, the ordinary sequence of life's event - they are just as important, just as much in need of God's healing love and care as life's crises and glories. For ours is a God whose concern is with *all* of our lives *all* of the time. To God, as we experience the revelation in Jesus of Nazareth, nothing is trivial, nothing unimportant.

And now this last word - Jesus thinks of us before we think of him. The evangelist records no word from Mary on this occasion. She stands before the cross a silent figure only to discover that even in death Jesus was more concerned with what he could give to her than what she could bring to him. And beyond that insight into the heart of God, we cannot go.

God's concern for us always outruns and outreaches our concern for God. Here is the abiding meaning of this third word from the cross. And what a magnificent assurance for living it is! If our relationship with God were on a cash and carry basis, if we could count upon God's attention only in response to our attention, how impoverished and empty our lives would be. If God's favors to us were only the return of our favors to God, how little of God any of us would have in our lives.

But this is not the case. God never forgets. God never grows indifferent. The initiative, the first word is always from God. Do not blame God for being cheap in goodness or compassion. Rather blame ourselves for being blind to the clear signs of goodness and compassion and the tokens of love which crowd upon our lives from every side. For He who on the cross could not forget his mother can and will never forget us - his sisters and brothers!

4th Word from the Cross

Text: Matthew 21:33-46 - "My God, My God, Why Hast Thou Forsaken Me?"

Is it possible to stand at the cross, listen to these words and not feel it marks the end of humankind's one last slender hope? The man, who for three years has preached trust in God, the burden of whose message has been a faith in the loving heart of the most gracious God, is dying. And, in his last moments on earth he is apparently unable to practice what he has been preaching.

For the entire world it looks as if, at the decisive moment, the faith of Jesus of Nazareth failed. And, if that is true, then our last hope vanished with his words. If at the point of agony and suffering Jesus himself was not able to keep his faith and his trust unbroken, what hope can there be for ours? If climbing Calvary was more than his faith could take, what must become of ours when we climb our much less severe Calvaries?

Yet, though what we have said remains true in the realm of theory, I do not believe most of us really feel that way when we hear these words. For whatever intellectual disappointments and frustrations we may feel at having our deepest questions about life unanswered are more than lost in our feeling of kinship with the man who could speak such words as these. Whether he got his answer or not, at least here is someone who has shared the experience of my human situation down to the very core.

We can admire and worship the man who in agony of crucifixion says, "Father, forgive them, for they do not know what they do." But as we admire and adore, we must do it from a distance because we understand that nothing in us is capable of that selfless reaction to suffering. But the man who cries out in pain: "My God, My God, why hast thou forsaken me?" is heart of our heart, mind of our mind, and blood of our blood. He has entered the darkest mystery of human life, the mystery of defeated goodness and victorious evil, the mystery of human lostness and abandonment. Standing by his cross, we recognize him as the one who has shared the tragedy of uncertainty in human life to the last full measure.

But, we may ask, "Does not that fact only make the situation worse?" Does not the fact that Jesus of Nazareth, better than anyone else, knew what loneliness and desertion and despair are, only deepen tragedy? For if he knew them so well, why did he not show us the answer to them? Experiencing our human loneliness and perplexity so keenly, he should have been able to provide us with the solution for them. Life involves us in enough situations in which we ask why, never finding an answer. But to discover Jesus sharing our place of darkness and uncertainty unable to find an answer to *why*, is almost the final tragedy

It may draw us to him; it may make us more aware of our common humanity; it certainly heightens the pathos of these last hours on Calvary. But, it leaves us with the riddle of humanity unsolved. Over all our innocent suffering, all our undeserved pain, all our unmerited sorrow, Jesus of Nazareth or no Jesus of Nazareth, there is still written the unanswered question, "Why?"

And yet, you know, I rather think the question, at least in the form in which Jesus put it, contains its own answer. Of course, we know it is a quotation from the 22nd Psalm. Every Jewish boy raised and nurtured on the Psalms. They were a stable diet item in their education. Jesus, therefore, would have been as familiar with the 22nd Psalm as we are of the 23rd. Was he quoting it here, perhaps even quoting the entire Psalm to himself as an act of prayer and devotion, though those standing by only caught this, its opening verse? Or was this cry from the cross no quotation at all, but something born of anguish and desolation of his own heart at the moment?

Well, I do not pretend to know the answer to these questions. But, whether a quotation or a question, the important thing to see is that these words answer the very question they ask, offer the only possible solution to the problem they put, "*My* God, *my* God, why hast thou forsaken me?"

We do not need to spend time describing what Jesus felt when he spoke these words. Though to an infinitely smaller degree, we have all known the feeling. We have it whenever we have been asked to shoulder burdens greater than we can bear, greater than we deserve to bear, whenever we feel some situation of suffering, our own or that of someone we love, is totally and absolutely undeserved. Above all, it comes over us when we feel that in this place of pain God doesn't care, God offers no help.

God has turned away and forgotten. That was what Jesus of Nazareth felt at this moment. We know what he felt for we have felt it too and we have asked the very same question.

4th Word from the Cross

          William P. Anderson

But is it a question? I have known people who in difficult times have cried out, "Why?" "Why is this happening to me?" A husband loses a wife, a mother loses a child, someone else loses sight, another hearing. And instinctively the question which comes to their lips is "Why?" Why should life be so unfair? Why should the universe be so cruel and unfeeling? Why should fate be so bitter? So certain are we that the world must be rational, that life must operate in terms of justice as we understand it, that when something irrational or unjust occurs, we are determined to track down the reasons for it, certain there must be some reason.

And I can see how we, seeing Jesus of Nazareth hanging on his cross and hearing him speak these words, would say, "See, even Jesus himself was finally forced to ask why! And even Jesus went out of this life without getting an answer! What can there be in his gospel for me?"

Yes - but this is to misread the story. Jesus hanging in death on his cross did not ask why. At least he did not ask it in the way in which we do. He did not fling out his question to an impersonal and unfeeling universe. He did not question the rationality of life or the justice of fate. That is the first great difference between his question and ours. When we ask why, we address the question to life or fate or to the universe, almost as though we believed life were some kind of calculating machine that should ring up happiness for the good and misery for the evil. And when in our opinion the results get mixed up - the good get misery and the evil get happiness - then it is time to question the operation of the machine, the time to ask *why*!

But if we ask why in that way we can never get an answer. To ques-

Part IV - The Redemptive Work of Jesus of Nazareth

tion what happens to us on the basis that it never ought happen to us is to ask a question better not asked, since it has no answer. Jesus, hanging on his cross, did not ask why, addressing his question to fate, luck, or the rational structure of the universe. He put his question to *God*! And that begins to make it a different question.

What is so different about it? Have not many people in their distress and despair asked, "Why did God do this to me?" "What have I done that God should treat me so?" What difference does it make whether they complain about the rationale of the universe or complain about the logic of divine purpose? Changing the terms doesn't bring the answer any nearer, does it?

Still, however, we have not got the question straight. Jesus did not say, "Why did God forsake me?" True, that is *our* question, but it is the wrong question. It is wrong because it indicates that in our thinking and believing, God is really a third party, somewhere on the outside of our living. We talk about God, read about God, listen to sermons about God and even occasionally believe in God.

But we believe in God the way we believe in the North Pole or the Taj Mahal. God is something we have heard about, read about. We know God is there, all right. But God is something we have never seen or known, i.e. we have no first-hand knowledge, no personal acquaintance. But if that were the only God Jesus had known, the first touch of the nails in his flesh would have made him an atheist. "Why does God do this to me?" is about as useful a question as asking what kind of toothpaste the Queen of England uses. For in either instance we are talking about someone so far away that any real knowledge about them is virtually impossible. Jesus,

4th Word from the Cross

hanging on the cross, did not question God as a third party, an outsider, a remote stranger, but *my God*. And because he put the question that way, it contained its own answer.

"My God, My God, ..." is a very different question from "Why has God forsaken me?" Even there in that place of darkness, despair and anguish, Jesus did not speak about a God *of* whom he had already he and *in* whom he had been led to believe. Even on Calvary, Jesus spoke with a God whom he personally knew and personally trusted ... not *God*, but *my God* ... not "why has he?" but, "why have *you*?" Even though he questioned God's ways, failed to grasp God's purpose, was unable to fathom God's activity, of this one thing he was certain, of this one thing he would not let go - this darkly mysterious God was still *his God*. *My God*! Never once did he permit even the most dire circumstances make God a stranger or an enemy. Even in loneliness and forsakenness, *my God*.

And here is the reason why this apparently darkest moment is really one of the brightest, why this word of despair which we think contains no answer actually contains the only answer that will hold against all doubts and all questions. No one will deny that the life of any one of us will contain, if it has not already done so, many hard moments, many difficult problems, many strange events. They are the raw materials out of which our lives must be made, whether we like them or not.

In the face of these things there are only two answers that can finally satisfy. The whole panorama of life is one gigantic fairy tale told by an idiot and the story of our lives has no more meaning than the scrawling of a baby - either that, or *my God* - difficult to understand, hard to follow, uncompromising in the demands this God places on us, but always known, always *my God*! It must be one or the other!

If it be the first, then let us light our candles and go out into the dark alone as bravely as we can, knowing that sooner or later a breath of chill air will snuff out its flame forever. But, if it be the second, remember that though life may sweep everything else away from us, so long as we can keep this elemental creed we can go on in hope. My God, not the God of the universe, not the God of the philosophers, not the God of the minister or the theologians, nor of my father or mother or my Sunday school teachers, but *my* God!

We cannot question fate. It is completely arbitrary and knows no human law. Today it does one thing, tomorrow another. What can we say? We cannot question the God of the Universe, the vast and unknowable being who spins the stars like tops and spreads out galaxies like blankets. That God is too vast for my tiny mind to comprehend. How could I possibly think that such limitless intelligence heeded my queries?

But we can question our God, not because we have the right to answers, not because God owes us anything whatsoever, but because this is *my God* whom I know and whom I trust, and whom I love. Whenever we question this God, we know we shall always receive an answer which, though it may not at the time solve the superficial riddles posed by our intelligence, will always meet those deeper needs posed by our hearts. Here is the only satisfying answer to life's troubling questions - to have the faith to bring them to a God who is personally known, personally trusted and personally loved. This God will make the way plain!

4th Word from the Cross

5th Word from the Cross

Text: John 19:28 - "I Thirst".

Seven times Jesus spoke as he hung upon the cross. But of the seven words he spoke here is the only one you and I could have said as well. Who of us, in the torment of crucifixion, would have called upon God, even to ask why we were being forsaken by him? However, what is expressed here is a need so human that any one of us could have spoken it. This word has nothing to do with religion, morality, or character, but entirely with sheer physical need! *I am thirsty!*

And who would not have been thirsty hanging there for three hours beneath a blazing Eastern sun while his life's blood ebbed away? I understand that of all the needs of the human body, thirst is far and away the most agonizing. Human beings can endure hunger for a fairly long period of time. It is amazing how much physical pain the human body can take. But thirst is like a consuming fire. The most devastating, the most intense agony any person can know is to feel his or her tongue thicken and throat become parched for lack of water. *"I Thirst!"*

It should not surprise us, then, that sooner or later there would come from the lips of Jesus this cry of human need. The surprise comes only when we set this whole scene in the context of our faith in and about Jesus as the Christ. If, as some maintain, Jesus was a man and simply a man, albeit the finest and fairest of all humanity, who died a martyr's death on Calvary, then even though his world is touching in its pathos, it does little more than remind us poignantly of the suffering he endured before he died. If Jesus was simply human there would be little more to say about these words. What message would there be in these two words, which simply draw attention to the fact that crucifixion is a very painful way to die.

However, if Jesus was and is what our faith claims and asserts - the one in whom the *fullness of God dwelt* - the translation into human personality of the divine presence and mind, as well as the divine heart - then even these two words glow with meaning and shine brightly with significance. Consider how far they take us into the inmost character of our God. Without doubt we all realize how many words of our language are symbolic, so that the selfsame word will suggest very different things to different people.

Well, what does the single, yet all important word *God* suggest to you? What picture does it call to your mind? There would be some whose immediate vision would be of some old man with a long white beard sitting on a big throne with angels hovering around. Some would see in their mind's eye one pictures of the good shepherd once so popular in Sunday School material. Some would get no picture at all, only a vague impression of what somebody once called an "oblong blur."

But, how many, I wonder, would see - when they heard the word God - a man nailed to a cross, murmuring with his parched lips, "I Thirst?" Yet this is precisely the picture of God presented to us in this scene. Each of these past phrases of Jesus of Nazareth is a precious photograph of the mind and heart of God. But this phrase is a picture which has nothing to do with religion, morality or character, but with sheer physical need. Of course, that is certainly true. But the fact that the gospel presents us a picture of God in a position of pure physical need *has everything to do*

5th Word from the Cross

with religion. The fact that at the center of our faith we find not some figure of remote and awful deity, not some super heroic person, not some discarnate spirit who lives beyond human pain, but One divine enough to forgive and human enough to be thirsty - that fact makes our faith unique.

If we do nothing else with it, I hope we can make this picture of God vivid and real. J. B. Phillips little book, *Your God is Too Small*, presents an analysis of the ways in which we must ask the appropriate question, and we ask it now in all seriousness, looking right at the one who said, "I thirst," Is our God "too big?" A ridiculous question? How can you have an idea of God that is too big when eternity is not enough to contain God? How can God be too big when, if we think at the outermost bounds of infinite space, we will have only touched the hem of God's garment? Well, all that is true. But it is still possible to have a God who is too big for the intimate and personal needs of individual lives.

Would you not agree? Is this not what has happened to so many people? It is not that we do not believe, of course we do! But between the belief and the heartaches, pains, problems and issues of life, there is such a wide - a very wide - gulf. The problem has to be a really big one before we let God in on it. When there is a death in the family, some natural catastrophe, war or rumors of war, then we think our problem has reached sufficiently large proportions to be of interest to God.

However, when it comes right down to us, moments of that sort are rare. And between them, life is filled with countless petty details, small questions, minor aches and pains which never see the healing light of God's presence. Part of this, of course, is the result of our strange idea that we are competent for these things and need no help, often resenting it when offered. But I am also sure that God is too big, too far away, to be interested or to care.

That is not the case! We must strike these images and misconceptions of God from our minds and realize this is not the God of the gospel, but a pathetic idol, the worship of which will cut us off from the peace, joy, courage, and hope we need and can most certainly have.

Here is the God of the gospel: a poor, pathetic dying man who pleads for a little water to moisten his cracked and burning lips. Call it an incredible picture is you like, a daring picture, or even a silly picture. Call it anything you please. But you can never stand at the cross, hear this word, and say that the God of the Gospel is impervious to human suffering, unconcerned about human pain, too big to be bothered with human need. We may go through life thinking of God as a blind and unpitying force in the sky. But here at the cross we are brought up short to learn - *it is not so*. In the words of the poet William Blake:

Till our grief is fled and gone
He doth sit by us and moan.

That is the God of the Gospel, caring for every human need because Jesus of Nazareth, the Christ, has shared every human need, even the simplest and most elemental of all - *"I thirst!"*

There is a second feature to the God of the Gospel which comes out of this word from the cross, namely, the sheer honesty of this scene as compared with so many shams and pretensions about life in which we so commonly indulge ourselves. As we minister to others, we spend a great deal of time with people in their pain - whether physical or the deeper

5th Word from the Cross

afflictions of the mind and spirit. Out of such experiences, we are often led to consider ways to meet these situations of suffering and pain.

Sometimes we try the *silver-lining-in-the-cloud* approach and try to persuade ourselves and our friends things are really not as bad as they seem. You know, sort of the kind of Job's comforter who is always telling you how much worse things could be. We minimize suffering, decorate death, and anesthetize pain until these realities are all but recognizable. This is all the religion many people know, the ability to pretend their way out of trouble. Cheer up; it is not as bad as it might have been.

Or there are those who meet life's hardships by way of the Stoic. They bite their lips, grit their teeth, tense their bodies, and plunge ahead. There must be no tears, no sighing, and no stopping to ask questions, no show of weakness. There are those who think the highest form of religion is never to let anyone suspect you have the slightest emotion, even in the most terrible moments of life.

If under extreme pressures they can maintain their dogged and sullen self-control, they think they have accomplished a mighty wonder. Though they may never have thought the matter through, their attitude reveals what they think about pain and suffering - they are simply to be endured. Their hero is the person who never opens her or his mouth, but like a dumb animal bears whatever burdens life puts upon them.

Do you see anything like this at the cross? Jesus is in pain. He does not pretend. There is about Calvary a rugged honesty that cannot fail to impress, whatever your religious convictions. Here is no pretending things are not as bad as they may seem. Here is no silly effort to find a silver lining in the cloud. Here is no deluded attempt to dismiss pain as imaginary or sorrow as unimportant. Here is suffering in all of its savage reality. "I thirst."

By the same token, here are no mock heroics, no false bravado. Hanging on the cross, Jesus does not hold back. Sure, he restrains his own sense of suffering until he has thought of others, his tormentors, his companions in death, his mother. But then, when the awareness of his own agony overwhelms him, he allows no false pride to hold it back, no sense of shame to keep it in. "I thirst." Frankly, honestly, unashamedly - "*I thirst.*"

I suppose that really does not take us very far with this terrible problem of our humanity, the problem of sin, pain and suffering. But I wonder whether it does not take us much farther than we realize. Come right down to the bedrock of the gospel and what do you find? A God who says: Cheer up, it's not as bad as you think? A God who bids us to keep a stiff upper lip, since it will soon be over? No, a God who sharing the pain and suffering of our suffering cries "*I thirst.*"

Here at the cross there are no sentimental pretenses, no mock heroics, no effort to make us angels or super humans, but an honest facing of all the facts of human existence in all their grim reality. A God who avoids the suffering of life would not interest me. A God who bid me be a hero when I am a coward could not help me. But a God who has honestly faced and felt the same suffering - that God I can follow. I may not know where it will all come out. But I at least have a guide I can trust - having been where I must go.

Isn't this the power of the Christian faith? It presents to us in Jesus

5th Word from the Cross

of Nazareth a God not too big to care and not too far away to know. The only God who can meet our need is the God who has honestly known our need. If the gospel presented me with a God who wrote prescriptions for human conduct and human need for the safe haven of heaven, I would *not* be a person of faith - certainly not a minister. But when it pictures a God who offers no prescriptions, no panaceas, but simply goes the way I (we) must go and gives the simple command to take up the cross and follow, my spirit stirs and starts up in eager recognition. This God who shares my need can meet my need.

For I too thirst. George Meredith has a poem which contains these lines which are most appropriate here:

Ah, what a dusty answer gets the soul

When hot for certainties in this our life.

We thirst for certainty. We thirst for assurance. We thirst for meaning and significance. We thirst for peace and contentment. Our hearts are hot and dry and sometimes grow so parched we think we can no longer stand the pain. Here at the cross are no easy answers, no easy speeches, and no quick solutions. But here is the One, Jesus of Nazareth, the Christ, who has opened the way to the waters of healing.

6th Word from the Cross

Text: John 19: 23-30 - "*Tetelestai*" or "It is finished!" And just what was finished?

The meaning of this word from the cross is rather uncertain if we look no further than the word itself. Just these three words (one in Greek) taken by themselves could constitute a very pathetic yet very human cry of weakness and defeat. It is finished. It is over with now – the suffering, the pain, the scorn. Death will soon draw its merciful curtain across the scene. There are no more burdens to be borne. There is no more pain to be suffered, no more torment to be endured. The powers of death have done their worst. *It is finished.*

Yes, and more than life itself is finished. Finished are the dreams and hopes with which he had once enthralled the multitude. Finished is the teaching that had once rung with authority. Finished is the mad career that just a few days earlier had drawn excited hosannas from hundreds of hearts. Finished is that kingdom, the coming of which, he had proclaimed so confidently. To what other conclusion may we come when a man who claimed to be a king hangs there like a bat nailed to a barn door? At least he had the wit to see it himself, the courage to admit the shattering illusions before he died. *It is finished!*

It would be perfectly possible on the basis of these three words to conclude that this was the way in which Jesus of Nazareth took his leave of life, gladly accepting the end, when it came, as a merciful release, meekly bowing his head to breathe his last breath. And much as we could have wished the end to be something different, what can we say? What can we say indeed but that at the last, as with all of us, the world proved too much for Jesus of Nazareth as well? *It is finished!*

But if we look a little beyond these three words, we will see that such was not the case at all. For one thing: only the gospel of John records this word. "It is finished!" The other three evangelists do not tell us what Jesus said at this point in the story. But all three of them record the fact that just before he died, he cried with a "loud voice." And by the words they use, they clearly indicate what they mean.

For this "loud voice" is exactly the phrase which is used in Greek to indicate a victor's shout; a triumphant cry, such as might rise from the throat of a runner who was first to cross the finish line in a race, such as might escape from the lips of a tired but happy wrestler who had won a difficult match. John apparently understood the words which the other three had heard only as a victor's shout. But putting the two accounts together makes it clear that these words were not whispered weakly as a last sad farewell to life, but shouted triumphantly as the victor crossed the goal.

But more than that, there is the word itself which came from his lips. In Greek, as we have pointed out, it is not three words, which might mean one of several things, but a single word which can mean one thing and one thing only, *Tetelestai. Finished! Accomplished! Achieved!* Here is no weak admission that, thank God, it is all over now. Here is the triumphant assertion that the job which was to be done has been completed. The mission that was assigned has been accomplished. In spite of incredible difficulties, in spite of almost insurmountable barriers, he has done it. Now let them say what they will, do what they may. They can neither injure nor destroy what he has completed. The word which he chose is rich with purpose and the *tense* he chose indicates the completion of that purpose. *It is finished!* With every flag waving proudly, with every banner still flying defiantly, the ship has been brought safely into port.

Perhaps you have had the good fortune to have heard the alto aria *"It is finished!"* in J. S. Bach's *Passion According to St. Matthew.* It begins with a setting of the words which is almost so low that it is almost a sob. You can hear the sorrow of humanity in it. But J.S. Bach was too good a theologian, too keen a person of faith, to let it stop there. Immediately the trumpets sound the note of victory and the solo continues: "The Lion of Judah has conquered!" That is the only way in which these words are rightly understood. Even while sobbing sounds, the trumpets of victory echo over it. The Lion of Judah has conquered. *It is finished!*

But now, exactly what was finished? Our original question still stands, even though we know the manner in which he spoke these words. What was finished? His life, to be sure. But what had he accomplished, what had been completed with the ending of his life? What was this goal the achievement of which gave Jesus of Nazareth such a conviction of victory as he died, transforming his very death into a triumph?

Certainly there are many ways in which we could answer that question. To be even more certain, there are many answers to that question which lie beyond the poor power of our minds to grasp and understand. But no one who has studied the life of Jesus even casually can fail to perceive that he was a man with a mission. Even as a boy of twelve he was conscious of God's mission in his life. And in the more mature years of his ministry, God's business was the motive for every word that he spoke and every deed that he did.

It was God's business that took him through Galilee preaching the kingdom and righteousness of God. It was God's business that moved him with compassion when he saw the multitude. It was God's business that led him to heal the sick and forgive the sinner. It was God's business that brought him willingly to Pilate's judgment hall. It was God's business that

6th Word from the Cross

made him stumble up Calvary with heavy cross. It was God's business that nailed him to that tree. And now it was God's business which he had completed with his victorious cry. "*It is finished!*"

And what was this business? We used to say that it was the saving work of Jesus in both his life and his death to bring people back to God. I surely would not wish to dispute the validity of that statement. However, I do think and believe that it contains the deepest truth about Jesus of Nazareth. More profoundly and deeply still, it was his business to bring God to humanity for in Jesus of Nazareth truly do we see the *humanity of God* and when we see the humanity of God, we also experience the deep, rich *love* of the very same God! - which is for *all* humanity!

An extreme statement in light of the fact that God has never left us. True! But what happened all through his life, climaxed by his death on the cross, was not just that Jesus led us back from the wasteland of our living to the old familiar place where God had been waiting all along. In Jesus of Nazareth, God, lovingly and personally, came right into the wasteland of our living, there to live, there to die. If it was our *failures* that kept us from finding God, very well, God would come right into the midst of our failures and dare the consequences. If it was our *pride* that kept us from our God, very well then, God would come right into the midst of our pride and takes its penalty. And this cry marks the last possible point God could reach in so dangerous a venture. For not even love can go further than dying.

I say it was a dangerous venture. To come with the errant and yet remain free, to be with the doubting and yet not dare give way to doubt, to be with the hateful and yet never fall victim to the control of hate - that sounds like a difficult if not impossible task. But that was the task Jesus of Nazareth had now finished. In terms of human personality, he had drawn the likeness of God for human beings without once blurring the lines or distorting the picture.

Anyone can speak about God in the quiet of a church or the calm of a study hall, speculating as to the nature of God, theorizing about God's character or attributes. But Jesus lived the life of God in all the heat and dirt, the blood and tears of our human situation without one betrayal of his mission, one failure in his task. One word of doubt, one answer of hatred, one show of weakness, one surrender to some lesser goal, and Jesus would have become a failure, presenting a false god to the human heart and mind.

But that had not happened, not even in the pain and agony and weariness of these last three hours. *Finished!* In Jesus of Nazareth, God has found us. In Jesus of Nazareth, we have found God. What matters that it cost him his life? It was worth it to be able to show humanity a finished sketch, in lines which they could not possibly misread, of the heart and mind of God.

We must also say that we wish something more of this note could be found in our understanding of the cross. So much of it is so weakly sentimental, the shedding of pious tears for the poor Redeemer and what he did there. We should save our tears for ourselves. Calvary is no wailing wall. It is history's most terrifying battleground. The powers of hell, of death, of estrangement, there unleash against him the whole arsenal of their weapons, those same weapons with which they have defeated us time and again. But they cannot defeat him. They cannot capture him as they

6th Word from the Cross

have captured us. Alone he stands against them and drives them beaten from the field. Look up at the cross; brush away the tears. Sing the glorious battle! Praise my heart the wondrous victor! *Tetelestai; it is finished!*

But now a postscript as it were. In the deepest sense of the word, it *is* finished. But in a lesser, though not unimportant sense, it is *not* finished. And that is precisely why we meditate upon the experience of the love of God at Calvary. For even though the sketch has been drawn, the picture drawn and painted, completely and finally, the battle won once and for all, in all the turmoil and confusion of our living, it is so easy to forget, to wander, to lose the vision and its assurance.

We need to see not just once but often the love of God hanging triumphantly on a cross. With all of our doubts and fears, we need to be assured again that God loves the world. We need some tangible token that all this is not somebody's hopeful guess, some empty preachment, but *burning reality*. That is why we take bread and break it, life the cup and drink it. This is my body broken for you. This is my blood shed for you. The God who found us in Jesus of Nazareth will never leave us. The love which grasped us at Calvary will never let us go. The victory of the cross is true today, tomorrow and forever!

Tetelestai: It is finished!

Amen and Amen!

7th Word from the Cross

Text: Luke 24:36 - "Father, into thy hands I commend my spirit."

There is not one of the seven last words of Jesus which contains stranger contrasts than this, the seventh and the last. Here in this final word there is pathos and power. There are tears, but there is also triumph. And if we really are to have a full picture of this last moment in the earthly life of Jesus of Nazareth, we must seem them both.

For if we see pathos with power, tears without triumph, then the death of Jesus becomes nothing but history's great tragedy, a sad song that must be played throughout in a minor key. And if we see power without pathos, the triumph without tears, the death of Jesus becomes nothing but a piece of divine play-acting, completely unrelated to the suffering and sorrow of our human lives. It is only when we see both that we understand how the death of Jesus can be what the Christian faith has always asserted - an even in which God shared the misery of our human existence to the full and by his sharing redeemed it into glory.

Let me start by calling your attention to something which at first glance may not seem to be very important. This last sentence which Jesus spoke is, with the exception of a single word, another quotation from the Psalms. The fifth verse of Psalm 31 reads: "Into thy hands I commend my spirit." To that quotation Jesus added the single word "Father."

In itself there would be nothing unusual about such a quotation. For the Psalms were both the hymnal and prayer book of the Hebrew faith. There was hardly any young person in Palestine who had not committed them to memory as part of their religious education. In times of great exaltation or of deep distress, various words of the Psalter would naturally come to mind as the finest expression of the hearts deepest feelings. Once before this, you may recall, Jesus had quoted from another Psalm when he cried out, "My God, My God ..." It need occasion no surprise, there-

7th Word from the Cross

fore, that once again and for the last time he fell back upon the Psalms to express what was in his heart.

But there is something more about this word from the cross. Much as many of us were taught to say our bedtime prayer, "Now I lay me down to sleep ..." every Hebrew child was taught to say, "Into thy hands I commend my spirit." That very Friday night in countless homes in Palestine when mothers had tucked their little ones in their beds and blown out the lights, they would hold their hands and listen while little lips formed this prayer: "Into thy hands I commend my spirit."

Some thirty years earlier, in such a home in Nazareth, time after time Mary kissed her son good-night and then listened while he said his evening prayer: "Into thy hands I commend my spirit." Now that same son, grown to manhood, climaxing his ministry on a cross, can find no better way to take farewell of life than that which he had learned at his mother's knee: "Father, into ... !"

There is something infinitely moving in that picture - and equally instructive. It brings the cross down from those theological heights where so often we isolate it to our level of understanding. In his final moment of suffering, Jesus spoke not some lofty discovery of the mature religious mind, not some bit of esoteric wisdom to be shared only by the few, but a childhood prayer, very likely the first prayer he had ever learned, one that had stayed with him through the years and now at the end was still able to nourish his being.

The shadows have lengthened and the evening has come. The busy world is hushed, the fever of life is over, and his work is done. The wheel has turned full circle. Did he in those last moments see once again the old familiar home in Nazareth, the face of his mother bending over him, as like a tired child he rested his weary head? "Father into thy hands I commend my spirit."

There is, as I have stated, something instructive here as well. Let me call attention to it. The religious forms and experiences of our adult lives are certainly important, as they deepen, strengthen and confirm the faith we have learned at home, in churches and elsewhere. But nothing is of greater consequence for our spirits than the first religious impressions of childhood. These we almost never lose. Time may change their shape, alter their form, and deepen their meaning. But time will never erase them. More than anything else they will be the things to which we return when skies are dark and the going is hard. The very first things we teach our children about God are the things they will remember the longest. You may think their little minds do not grasp or understand. You may wonder why it is necessary to both with religious education at all when its content is so much greater than they can comprehend. Here is the answer. Even when everything else disappears, this remains. Jesus' last word from the cross was this little prayer he had learned at his mother's knee. "Father, into thy hands I commend my spirit."

We have spoken of pathos. We have seen tears. Now for the power and the triumph, for there are truly here as well. And it would be a pity if the tears and the pathos made them obscure to our hearts and minds. In one sense these words are a prayer. In another sense, like every good prayer, they are a creed. They are Jesus of Nazareth's final conviction about life and its meaning, hammered out in the agony of a cross. The last word is not simply his farewell to mortality. The last word is his last word on

7th Word from the Cross

what life is and what life truly means.

That last word, that creed that final assertion can be summed up in this: our lives are held gently but firmly in the strong grasp of One who is not only Intelligence but Love.

Moreover, this last word from the cross may very well be the most impressive thing Jesus ever said. To be sure, this was not the first time he had said it; it was not the first time he declared this was his Father's world. The "Sermon on the Mount," for example, echoes with that glad assertion. However, it is one thing to say it where lilies wave and crowds gather, where the sky is blue and the sunlight sparkles, with a heart so filled with joy that God is Love and that God's hand is upon all we do, say, and experience. But, please forgive, I believe in that setting I could have said the very same thing.

But there is another mount. Here are no lilies, but thorns. The crowds have not come to listen, but to mock. The sun has been swallowed up in darkness and the sky is heavy and dark. The heart is no longer filled with joy, but bursting with sorrow. And yet this cross is a "sermon on the mount" more telling than anything he had preached before. In this sermon, he preaches not with words, but with his life. Nevertheless, the text remains the same, unchanged! "Father, into Thy hands I commend my spirit."

This makes this "sermon on the mount" unforgettable. Here was no evidence of a Father - the sun grown dark with mystery, the body aching, bleeding, and sore, the cause deserted even by those who had professed it. Does this look like the handiwork of a Father or a cruel joke? Certainly, there is no hand of God present here. Where may we trace it on that bleak and desolate hill crowned with three crosses? Where would we find it in that grim murderous scene? It was not there, you say; was Jesus of Nazareth just making grandiose statements which simply were not true?

But that would be an erroneous conclusion! We know well enough that Jesus did not make statements of which he himself was not convinced. We know Jesus well enough that bluff and bravado were not in him. If in the darkness and death of Calvary he was still convinced his life was held in the grasp of an omnipotent hand, he said it because he believed it. He spoke it because he knew it.

Indeed, what are these hands of God that hold us? We seem to think God keep his hand behind his back, so to speak, never once interfering in the course of our lives or the direction of this world unless we should happen to decide God should. Then, in response to our demand we would like to see the heavens open and God's hand reach down to pick us up out of the dark valley and set us down once again in green pastures. After that, of course, we would like nothing better than for God to withdraw and let us alone until we think we have need again.

It is clear Jesus never thought that way about the hand of God. He never thought of God as a big law enforcer who came running whenever we blew the whistle. And certainly neither the scriptures nor our Christian faith sees God in this manner. The hand of God is not the strong arm of intervention which strikes out in massive retaliation against wrong-doers. Rather the picture is quite different.

In the darkness, confusion, mystery of our lives, the hand of God is something extended for us to grasp, for us to hold. Sometimes the path is rough. Sometimes the water is deep and cold. We may wonder why it should be that way. But it is that way and there is no better answer. Nevertheless, no matter how rough and dark the path, no matter how cold and deep the stream, there by our side, if we will just reach out to grasp it, is the hand of a powerful Love. And if there is anything in life and death of which we may be sure, it is this. That hand of Love is always there and will always be there.

We may not always know where we are going. We may not know how we will get there. But we can always know this: the hand of God is stretched out to us in all of its strength. Once we grasp it, God will never let us go - no, not even when we must enter the confidence that same hand that has led us all the way will lead us safely across and up into those eternal hills which shine in glory on the other side.

What then was the final creed of Jesus, his last conviction about human experience? For reasons which pass our understanding our lives contain materials which are rough and raw, and the only person who needs to be without the strong hand of God is the person who so chooses. If we put out our hand in faith, we shall always find God's hand grasping ours in love. Like little children afraid to climb the stairs in the dark unless their fathers take them by the hand, so we cannot find our way unless our Father grasps our hand as well. Once we feel that powerful hand supporting us, we can go on and not be afraid. We can run and not be weary. We can walk and not faint.

This last word from the cross is not dying man's philosophy of life, no mere echo of a childhood prayer. It is the secret of victorious living, to be renewed every day we live. Do we face problems we cannot even begin to solve? Into Thy hands! Do we experience sorrow we are sure we cannot bear? Into Thy hands! Is life with its many complications too much for us? Into Thy hands! Are we staring across the great sea of eternity wondering what lies on the other shore, wondering if there is another shore? Into Thy hands!

There is nothing in life or death, not even a cross, for which this word of confidence is not the answer. We cannot explain our hardships. We cannot find the reason for our troubles. We will never be able to live free in this world from them. But put our hand in the hand of God and we will always find a way through.

This is not *my* word to you, although my little experience in life tends to confirm it. This is the word of *one* who first learned this faith at his mother's knee, who proclaimed it gladly to the thronging people, who spoke it tenderly to hearts that were sore and perplexed, who tested it in the harsh experience of crucifixion, who used it to shatter the darkness, sin and death and let in the unquenchable light of life and love.

It is the word of Jesus of Nazareth, our Lord, and the Christ, guaranteed with his life's blood. For see, the hand stretched out to us in the darkness still bears the marks of nails. That is why this experience for us is not an ending, but most assuredly a beginning!

2. Some Poetic Reflections

THE OTHER SIDE

'Twas warm and uplifting
    as I walked beside the river wide

Wondering---is there a crossing, a bridge perhaps
    to take me to the other-side?

Unknown spectra there await exploration
    lifting my heart, soul and mind
Allowing my inner being complete adoration
    seeing how this world may be kind.

Whilst thinking thus, it came to me,
    my heart, spirit, mind singed and swelling,
God has put this within---announcing
    a forever journey for me.

But, I wonder, as I wander along the river-wide
    will I discover a bridge to the other-side?
Will my spirit be enlightened, will my heart be graced
    will God show me, life has a loving, meaningful side?

JESUS WEEPS IN LOVE AND COMPASSION
AND I WEEP WITH HIM

Jesus approached the great city of Jerusalem;
    as he came upon the city,
    in light of all he was, all he is,
    all he taught, all he did;
He weeps!

I look at this world, in the light and image
    of Jesus and I, too, weep!

Part IV - The Redemptive Work of Jesus of Nazareth

I weep for the poor, powerless, without influence
   in a world dominated by gold and silver,
   by stocks and bonds, bank accounts,
   by those in powerful positions.

I weep for the homeless, without shelter,
   without hope,
   seen as outcasts
   ---the misfits of society;

I weep for those possessing much in worldly things;
   yet impoverished in mind, soul and spirit;

I weep for the disenfranchised,
   who have been pushed to the edge of life,
   life without opportunity,
   life without meaning, purpose, direction.

I weep for this world, with all of its beauty,
   with all of its richness and grace,
   yet wallowing in hate, distrust, confusion and chaos,
   suffering pain and shallowness.

I weep for the rich,
   the powerful, the kingmakers,
   the influence brokers, the titans of this world,
   envied by many, but --- in reality,
   less than a shadow of
T.S. Eliot's Hollow Men,

2. Some Poetic Reflections

    William P. Anderson

Stuffed men,

    empty characters in a play

    with no-ending, hurrying, going nowhere,

    with nothing of Real Value

    in their blank minds,

    their cold, hardened, calculating hearts.

I weep for those who seem:

    so filled with life

    so powerful

    so radiant

    yet lonely

    even amidst the crowd,

living lives devoid of

    real meaning;

    cardboard figures on the chessboard of life,

    moving to and fro,

    riding every whim and

    fancy like a surfer

on the waves of the ocean,

    finding momentary---

    fleeting pleasure.

Alas, Alas, we may think and say,

    but, take heart, O Traveler on the road of life,

Jesus not only weeps,

Jesus gives Love,

Jesus gives inner power and insight,

    meaning and purpose to life,

Part IV - The Redemptive Work of Jesus of Nazareth

true purpose in a seemingly vacant world.

Truth in Life from the Source of Life,

Jesus gives the power to transcend

    loneliness,

    emptiness,

    meaninglessness

    shallowness.

The One Who we call the Christ

has shown us

    the way

    the light

    the truth

and has wrapped us in His Love---

    giving Himself for us,

Challenging us to share His Love---

    the essence of God's nature:

challenging us to be his Ambassadors---

    to be living images of His Life!

2. Some Poetic Reflections

Part V - A Christian View of Being Human

1. On Being Human

It would be wonderful if we could believe that God created the world, that when God takes an interest in us and is thinking higher thoughts about us. However, can we really believe the words of the scriptures concerning God's relation to humanity without doing violence to the integrity of our intellect? For, after all, the scripture says we were created out of the dust of the ground and we know human beings came into existence altogether differently. We know that life on this planet is billions of years old and that humans developed upward from animality in an unimaginably long process. Does not faith with its mythical, legendary conceptions occupy the short end of the seesaw against science, which has long put biological development in the place of these ancient, outmoded conceptions of creation - and done so by means of exact evidence?

This is how the question is commonly stated. But it seems to me that scientific doubt about belief in creation is based upon a completely erroneous way of putting the question. That is: I can either ask where humanity came from *biologically* and receive the answer that we have sprung from pre-human animal forms, or I can ask, *to what purpose* we are here, what are we intended to be, what the *point of our existence* is. If I ask the latter question, the answer I get from the scriptures is we are designed to be children of God, that we are intended for fellowship with one another *and* with God. It becomes apparent then that these two questions should not be mixed or confused. They are on two different levels. And, therefore, they do not express and *either-or* situation any more than it is a mutually exclusive *either-or* for me to say on the one hand *The St. Matthew*

Passion is a musical form of worship and, on the other, *The St. Matthew Passion* is a sequence of physically measurable sound vibrations. These two statements also are on different levels and, in their own particular way, both are true.

God-Consciousness?

Once we understand this clearly, we are at the following consequences. I do not offend against faith when I say that human beings developed from animality over millions of years. How can one truth, that of science, offend against another truth, that of faith? No, I offend against the faith when I dare to assert I can derive the essence of humanness, of human destiny, of the meaning of life, from this animal origin. For when I attempt to do this, the answer I arrive at is that we are *simply* a higher mammal; perhaps a beast of prey; but in any case determined by the instincts of food seeking, acquisition, and sex. Then world history would just be a separate chapter in zoology.

1. On Being Human

Human beings are different! The basic issue for humanity, that which sets humans on the path to *Homo Sapiens* (wise man) instead of *Homo Naturalis* (natural man) is this: human beings are born short on instinctive *know-how*. We are, so to speak, deficient in DNA knowledge, which is to say humans are *non-programmed* animals: the ones for whom life and meaning depend not on simple maturity, but on *instructed* maturity. We cannot simply grow up and be ourselves (wise humans - *Homo Sapiens*); we must grow up instructed, educated. The existentialist philosophers are correct when they argue that humans are the only species in creation whose existence precedes their essence. The essential nature of other species of life is programmed, instructed, built into the genetic structure. Ours is not! A tiger is always a tiger. It is born that way. It can never be anything but a tiger, and exactly that kind of tiger. This is not the case for humans. It is true at birth there is an *instructed* part laid down in human beings: their physical existence. But not *humanity, not mind, not language, not attitudes, loves, antipathies, sadness,* and *not religion.* All this - and all else which makes one *a person, a personality, a human being,* - is yet to be learned, yet to be created.

Human beings have self-consciousness and imagination. To say this is to say a person sees himself or herself. Humans see themselves as involved in a past, a present, and a future. I, for example, know myself to be myself. I am an *object* to myself. I can, at one and the same time, be both subject and object. I may not see myself exactly as others see me, but I definitely see myself, as do you. I see myself in consciousness present. Is this also not what the scripture writers had in mind when they declared human beings are "created in the 'image' of God?" Human beings are creative beings, self-transcendent beings, with unique possibilities for both good and evil, for constructive creativity, and even self-destruction. It is a marvelous, challenging, and dangerous responsibility, but one that is incumbent upon all humanity.

Evolution

And here we find religion. Human beings are the only species that *do* religion, or philosophy, the arts, the sciences, and all those unique things that contribute to culture and its growth and development. We are, in a sense, *co-creators*, with the Author of the Universe. Is it not to this end God caused humanity to emerge from the ranks of all other creatures and made humanity to be something unique? This idea is captured magnificently, poetically, and succinctly in the Genesis text when the writer says: "God ... breathed into [his] nostrils the breath of life; and [man] became a living soul." Here this earthly creature, still bound within universal creatureliness, which the scriptures present in the symbol of "dust from the ground," here, this pre-human still unformed substance,

1. On Being Human

was breathed upon by the breath of God, by the breath of another world and translated into that realm which we call *human life*. I have always felt Michelangelo's portrayal of the birth of humanity in his famous painting in the Vatican's Sistine Chapel, is a singularly profound expression of this story of human creation. Adam is already there; but he is in a sense not yet there, as a real human being. Adam is still a *candidate* for humanness. He lies half-erect, still in a dreamy stupor, though his face is turned toward the Creator in questioning expectation or anticipation. His leg is already taut, ready to rise, and all is prepared for him to rise up in the next instant and face God. Between these two moments, a miracle must occur - the miracle of the spark of the Spirit leaping from the outstretched finger of God, the Creator, to Adam the created. Without this miracle he would ever have remained an earthbound creature and would never have become the wanderer between the two worlds he was destined to become. Perhaps he may have been a higher creature, (how beautiful is Michelangelo's Adam even before he became a human being) but he still would have been something other than the one who would be privileged to become God's child and partner. Michelangelo portrays, most beautifully as only he could have done, the last moment of *pre-humanness*, and it is not until the next moment that Adam becomes human: a child, a neighbor, a brother, a love - the *imago Dei*, the image of God, and at the same time one of whom it "does not yet appear what he shall be." (I John 3:2) For God is not yet finished dealing with us and our history goes on - to the world's last moment and even beyond to eternity. In the thoughts of many great Christian thinkers, e.g. Irenaeus of Lyons, Gregory of Nyssa, and Teilhard de Chardin, just to cite a few, *we are always in the process of becoming* with the incarnate love of God reaching out to us, even as Michelangelo's God reaches out to Adam, drawing us ever closer to his inner being.

Part V - A Christian View of Being Human

Come On Baby Light My Fire

2. Human Inter-connectedness

One of the most well-known phrases in all of English literature is the phrase: "No man is an island, entire of itself;" the fame is no doubt influenced by its association with Ernest Hemingway cited it in his great novel *For Whom the Bell Tolls*.

The phrase itself comes from John Donne's *Meditation 17* written by the great poet and churchman in 1623. Donne was a poet, who had the gift of marvelous insight, a metaphysical thinker of great depth, and a writer whose rich imagery touched, and even yet touches, the hearts and lives of many in the English speaking world. Placing this phrase in the larger context from which it comes, we read:

> "No man is an island entire of itself; every man is a piece of the continent, a part of the main. If a clod be washed away by the sea, Europe is the less, as well as if a promontory were, as well as if a manor of thy friend's or thine own were. Any man's death diminishes me, because I am involved in mankind; and therefore never send to know for whom the bell tolls; it tolls for thee."

It is clear, of course, the tolling of the bell of which Donne speaks, is a tolling for one who has passed from this life to the next, a tolling that honored the life of one leaving our midst. But, poet, churchman, and theologian that he was, Donne cast more significant meaning and deeper understanding into those experiences and words. It relates to the very essence of the Christian faith, exploring and giving meaning to the inter-connectedness of this life we share with one another and with God. Donne's insights permit us to come to an understanding of not only who we are, but to whom we ultimately belong.

We pause and reflect on our lives with one another; we seek to explore our relationship with God in deeper, richer ways, we are more keenly aware that our relationship with God must find its way into more positive, creative, loving relationships with our fellow human beings. For it is in this way that we truly become more human, more truly bearers of the image of God in our lives. John Donne captured this profoundly when he points out that "any man's death diminishes me." Certainly then, the death of Jesus of Nazareth, the perfect human, *diminishes me absolutely!* If we have even the most limited understanding of this, we, in our frail and limited ways, will be enlightened in our love and concern for our fellow human beings, even those who are our foes and enemies. All this is possible for us as we move toward Jesus of Nazareth whose image is reflected in us as a gentle reality in our lives. The true joy of this experience is simply this: we catch a glimpse of what it means to be a child of God, a true human being and we, and the world, are never the same again for we have been touched by peace, compassion, and a love which can only come from the very being of God!

Jeepers Creepers!

2. Human Inter-connectedness

We are, as the gospel and John Donne suggest, every person - each one of us - a piece of the continent; we are, every man, woman and child, a piece with one another. We share in life's joys, as well as life's sorrows; we share in life's gifts, as well as its pain; we share in life's grace and love, because we have as our foundation - the Ground of All Being, even God; we have grace and love which enables us to extinguish the pseudo-power of hate; we have peace that overcomes all evil and passes all understanding. We have a life that is rich toward God and toward one another.

Go, share that with everyone, and you shall be more than fulfilled!

3. The Power of One

In the book, *Stone Soup for the World*, in a very brief story simply titled: "Starfish," the editor, Marianne Larned demonstrates the power a person may have. It is a story of a very young girl walking along a beach where thousands of starfish had been washed ashore during a violent storm. When she came to each starfish, she would pick it up and throw it back into the ocean. She had been doing this for quite some time when a man came up to her and said, "Little girl, why are you doing this? Look at this beach! You can't save all these starfish. You can't begin to make a difference!"

The little girl seemed surprised and a bit deflated. However, after a few brief moments, she bent down, picked up another starfish, and hurled it as far as she could into the ocean. Then she looked up at the man and replied simply, "Well, I made a difference to that one!"

The power of one is far greater than we imagine. Jesus of Nazareth, for example, was one man, but his life has affected billions of people over the past two millennia. His message of love, twisted, misconstrued, and rejected by many has yet become the standard for what it means to be human, what it means to be loving, what it means to have compassion. Like the little girl of the story who would neither be dismayed nor dissuaded by the indifference, the powerlessness of the many, Jesus of Nazareth gives us a *raison d'etre*, a reason for being. One person, living a life of love can make a difference; one person personifying in his or her life the high moral ground of Jesus of Nazareth, a life of service, a life of compassion and concern, can make a difference even in a world as hostile as ours today.

Something's Fishy Here

3. The Power of One

We can hurl hate into the ocean of God's love to be swallowed up and transformed; we can hurl abusive power into the ocean of God's strength and power to be crushed into nothingness; we can hurl indifference into the sea of God's goodness opening up the goodness, love and grace at the heart of every person and provide a foundation for life that will mirror heaven on earth; we can hurl the brute force of this world, present in so many nations and their leaders, into rivers of justice that flow from the fountain of God's being creating a world of peace, a world of harmony between nations, people of all races, and people of all religions. For our God is one, but One who is called and known by many names.

After World War II, Martin Niemoeller, a hero of the first World War and later a pastor in the Reformed Church of Germany as well as one who opposed the tyranny of Adolf Hitler, commented on the power we all have within us, a power which we often fail to use. Although he opposed the Third Reich and its policies, he felt he could have and should have done even more. And so he offered these now very well-known words:

> "In Germany they came for the communists, and I didn't speak up because I wasn't a communist. Then they came for the Jews, and I didn't speak up because I wasn't a Jew. Then they came for the trade unionists, and I didn't speak up because I wasn't a trade unionist. Then they came for the Catholics and I didn't speak up because I was a Protestant. Then they came for me, and by that time no one was left to speak up."

If each *one* of us will have courage to speak sharing the love of God and the grace revealed to us in Jesus of Nazareth, the Christ, the one will become many and the light of God's truth will dispel the evil, the hate, the prejudice of the world and we will indeed be one with God and with each other.

4. Some Poetic Reflections

FROM THE OTHER SIDE - A DOVE

A warm day
Refreshing
As I stride beside
The river wide.

Water flowing freely
Pristine, gentle
As it sweeps
Along the shore
Beckoning me to cross
To the other side.

The bird of love,
The dove, descends
Urging me "Come
Where you may truly be!"

Passing I wonder, rise to
The outer limits of my
Imagination and see -
A bridge standing before me
Moving my heart - stirring
Within a sense of glee.

Will anxieties be quelled?
Will hate? Will fear?
Sensing bewilderment
Gently swooping to me does
The dove of love appear,

Whispering softly, warmly,
"Come comfort, joy elation,"
Words from above and afar
"Not to fear, truly are
You loved my dear!"

A child of God you are
Welcomed to a place
Where you will be
Eternally loved! Forever free!

REFLECTIONS AT LONG INTERLAKEN

Newly fallen snow, cold, crisp
    blankets trees
    covers the forest floor
With sparkling beauty
    opening my heart
    lifting my spirit
Engaging my mind with
wonder and awe of
the brilliance of creation
A sight to behold -
    with beauty - with majesty
    beyond description

Part V - A Christian View of Being Human

Beautiful beyond description
    for certain, hidden
Round this beauty in all corners
      of the earth
Hidden in darkness
    are those without sight
    for nature
    for beauty
    for love
    for compassion

Are there some, perhaps
    the hopeful?
    the faithful?
Who with warm tender love
    deeds of kindness
    joyful hearts
Lift the spirits of those frozen in place
    those less fortunate
In a world too filled with itself
    to experience
    to feel
    To see
    reach out with
The beauty, love, and grace of God.

I think of these things each winter's day
    as I rise and survey the frozen

4. Some Poetic Reflections

waters of Lake Long Interlaken
Awaiting the day the crystal flakes of snow
    the depths of ice beneath the surface

Fade in the presence of a new day,
    a day of warmth,
    a day of sun,
    of leaves green and lush

The magnificence and majesty of
    new birth, regeneration
    a joyful new creation

As I look now at my lake - tranquil
    deep and dark
    in the dawning of this new day

I am thankful for the One
    who creates - for all who create
    who loves - for all who love
    who reach out to all - for all who reach out
With simple gifts - beautiful and free!

Part V - A Christian View of Being Human

Part VI - Christian Ethics and Religion

1. Christian Ethics and Religion

At the outset let me define *Christian Ethics* in the following way: Christian Ethics is a critical examination of the concrete relation between our commitment to Jesus of Nazareth and the multiplicity of commitments and loyalties of our individual and corporate existences, to the end that we may by our actions demonstrate a more faithful loyalty to our God.

To put it in a simpler form: Christian Ethics is a critical dialogue about our commitments and loyalties. Understood in this manner, ethics is principally a process of analyzing and reflecting on the multiplicity of our commitments and loyalties in light of our fundamental oath of allegiance.

When we view ethics primarily as a process of our critical thinking, we can reasonably distinguish it from *morality*. Ethics is *not* morality and morality is not ethics. While the two concepts are certainly interrelated, they are not necessarily synonymous.

Both terms: ethics and morality derive from a common root: the Greek word *ethos*. Ethos originally referred to, and meant, a dwelling or a stall. Its humble origin referred to a stall in which an animal was placed for both comfort and safekeeping. Thus ethos came to mean that which gives stability to life, whether the life be that of a human being or some other animal, e.g. a horse, cattle, etc. In this way ethos may be seen as the style or pattern of social intercourse which gives a community security and in which they may feel and be comfortable.

1. Christian Ethics and Religion

Gradually, a distinction grew up between the words *ethics* and *morality*. Even though common usage today may subvert that difference, there is no real reason to abandon it. On the contrary, we should salvage or recover this distinction between the two terms if we are to think and act ethically in the midst of our contemporary common life.

Let me propose a working definition for the term *morality* as it applies to our day-to-day actual conduct or to put it differently as it applies to our human behavior as it is guided by the most direct rules of action. I am, or course, referring to the *mores* of a particular society as they point to its conventional patterns of activity, those which are accepted, respected and followed, those which give security and stability to the people who live in a particular region of the world. Conceived in this manner, morality refers to such *rules* as: "Honesty is the best policy," and the consequent application by the person of that rule. It refers to the "person of good character," who is recognized and affirmed as being and doing the good. We refer to such persons as people of "high moral character." And further, we may assert a moral order or system is a collection of rules, guidelines, or patterns of life that people accept affirm or follow. These rules, policies, attitudes provide meaningful and dependable direction for the lives of the community. In his context a moral person or moral group is one that fits into the accepted pattern or style of life insofar as she or he or it is able.

Looking at it from this perspective, it is reasonable to argue most people are *moral persons.* Most people obey conventional laws. Most people live according to the dominant and received customary patterns of their sociological situation. They drive their cars under the speed limits (or perhaps slightly above). Normally men do not beat their wives nor do wives generally malign their husbands - in either hetero or homosexual relationships. Generally the rules of the game are followed in the business community and ballot boxes are not stuffed - although recently there has been more than a little *hanky-panky* attending the election process - but in general it all seems to work. In other words, people such as we have been describing give stability to a society, they preserve it from fragmenting anarchy; they respect the received tradition and for the most part abide by it without question. In this sense "morality" is the currency of everyday life.

However, people who live their lives in this way are not *necessarily* practitioners of Christian ethics. Let me cite a biblical example to illustrate: We all remember that the Pharisees of the 1st Century were *highly moral* persons. They received, affirmed and followed the conventional morality to a fault. They kept all the laws, even those, e.g. which demanded that blasphemers be put to death. They preferred that the laws be obeyed rather than a lame man be healed or a blind man have his sight restored on the Sabbath.

However, morality is not "ethics!" One theological ethicist put it this way: "Many churchman [sic] may indeed be moral, that is, zealous in upholding certain practical guidelines to righteousness that have been handed down out the recent past, but they are not ethically oriented viz., equipped to reflect on human responsibility in light of new demands on us, on the one hand, and of the theological principles of our heritage on the other." For the Christian person ethics is a *process* of examining our moral lives (and our immoral lives as well) in light of our commitment to Jesus of Nazareth - the Christ - in order to be more faithful.

The raw material for the ethical process is the individual and corpo-

1. Christian Ethics and Religion

rate lives we live. And ethics is a process that simultaneously is critical and nourishing of that common life. Ethics is thus the *midwife* of new moralities which are perhaps more adequate for a time, yet authentically true to basic commitments. As people of the Christian faith it is necessary for us to recognize that moral patterns must be re-framed sooner or later and that the requirements and claims of our common lives must be constantly reassessed in the midst of changing environments. It is clear that old patterns of life give way to new, that what once made for stability, security and comfort for many within a society may, if preserved uncritically, make for uncertainty, insecurity, and perhaps even lead to chaos for all. At the same time, it is incumbent upon us to recognize as well that there may well be individual practices and social customs that should/must be underwritten by one's fundamental ethical commitment.

Ethics is, therefore, an examination process in which we, as thinking Christian people, participate. It is an inquiry into our moral practices, our moral rules and our common life. Every generation is invited to share in this challenging process. This is particularly true for those of us who are loyal to Jesus of Nazareth. According to scripture, God's involvement with humanity is one of the most, if not the most, radical fact of human existence. It is so for it redirects us from death to life, from old comfortable patterns and habits to a new and changed pattern of life. It provokes radical self-examination, a search for life lived from its roots, from the One who is the ground of our being, the ground of life itself. It is this involvement of God with humanity that is the *time-bomb* for Christian decision-making. Such an involvement yields a *behavioral fallout* for all Christian people.

This critical ethical inquiry is not simply an *individual* responsibility, but a corporate one as well. It is an examination of myself as an individual actor and an actor in concert with others, in company with other thinking Christian people, and with those who do not confess a faith in Jesus of Nazareth or any other faith for that matter. Even our analysis and reflection about our common life together is carried on with others, as we seek to understand and respond to life in all of its tremendous richness and in all of its dimensions. We *ethicize* about our responsibilities as loyal citizens with other citizens. With our colleagues in the church we think about what we should do in terms of our loyalty to and with the community of believers; with our neighbors we wonder about what will contribute to a vital, fulfilling neighborhood. We, who call ourselves Christians, engage in such discourse to continue to become more faithful in our common life.

Ethics is also a *linking* device. It joins together in an explicit fashion our basic commitment and loyalty to Jesus of Nazareth and the many and variegated commitments and loyalties within the common life. It affirms that commitment to Jesus by itself is an abstraction: sentimental, empty language yielding conventional life. It recognizes, as well, that the common life we lead is by itself disordered and disfigured. It presumes the relationship between the two must be clarified, discovered or perhaps *re-discovered*. It is when these elements are brought together that sparks fly, that there is excitement that one begins to sense something of the dramatic nature, power, and love of the Christian faith. There is nothing abstract here for the conversation centers on our loyalties and our commitments. Examples and cases are concrete and very plentiful: gender, women's rights, race, ethnicity, the lack of meaningfulness in work, etc. These and others are the cases that confront and challenge us now, that cry for decisions and actions, which determine the quality and content of

1. Christian Ethics and Religion

our lives together as human beings. Ethics deals with concrete loyalties and actions, not with amorphous abstractions.

Finally, ethics is an intensely honest and practical inquiry. The goal of ethical inquiry is a more adequate and valid practice of the Christian life. It is not an exercise in cerebral gymnastics or simply a diversion from the normal daily round. It deals openly and frankly with life lived by human beings who decide and act every day. Any attempt to deal with those decisions and actions which glosses over the reality of the conflict of loyalties, and the intense ambiguity of moral decision is a snare and delusion. Yet the goal of ethics, as an examination of life, is that those decisions and actions may exhibit faithfulness to the love, the grace, and the goodness of God.

Christian ethics has to do with loyalties, with the issue of how we are to be loyal to God in the midst of the complexities and multiplicities of loyalties. It does not provide us with a list of rules as to what should be done. Dietrich Bonhoeffer was absolutely correct when he argued: "An ethic cannot be a book in which there is set out how everything in the world ought to be but unfortunately is not." (*Ethics*, p. 236) Ethics is a process of analysis and reflection, of examination, which helps to provide the raw materials whereby Christian people may understand their own lives more adequately and respond more faithfully to God's absolute claim in the midst of all the claims and demands laid upon us in our common life. Only as Christians engage in this process of ethical reflection does the self or the church approach the integrity that comes when all loyalties are ordered by a fidelity to the One who In Jesus of Nazareth shows faithfulness to and for us in the full range of the common life.

2. Some Poetic Reflections
REFLECTIONS AT THE CHURCH DOOR

I was hungry

and you formed a humanities club

and discussed my hunger.

                 Thank You!

I was imprisoned

and you crept off quietly

to your chapel

and prayed for my release.

                 Thank You!

I was naked

and in your mind

you debated the morality of my appearance.

                 Thank You!

I was sick

and you knelt

and thanked God for your health!

I was homeless

and you left me alone to pray!

                 O Thank You, again and again!

You seem so holy, so close to God

but I am still hungry

and lonely

and cold!

So---where have all your prayers gone?

What have all your prayers done?

And what does it profit anyone

to leaf through prayer books and pray

when the rest of the world

is crying for help?

What does it profit anyone

to leaf through the pages of scripture

when the rest of the world is dying?

Dying, simply wanting to be loved!

Lord, when will we ever learn?

When, O When, O Lord will we ever learn?

Sign, Sign, Everywhere a Sign ...

Part VI - Christian Ethics and Religion

Part VI - The Resurrection of Jesus of Nazareth

Without question the resurrection of Jesus of Nazareth is central to an understanding and practice of the Christian faith. In some ways it may be considered the *sine qua non* of our faith. One way of describing this thought, so critical to Christianity, is to view it in terms of its *significance* rather than attempting to justify its centrality to the faith with an appeal to its historical verifiability and veracity. From the perspective of the Christian faith, the resurrection is an activity of the One we claim as God and takes place in the life and work of Jesus of Nazareth, a first-century Palestinian Jew.

Because the significance of this act or event is of such importance to the Christian faith, as well as being of deep personal interest, I have chosen to explore, albeit briefly, at least some aspects of this significance. In the course of this brief reflection, these reflections are: 1) the significance for Jesus of Nazareth - the One we claim and call the Christ; and 2) the significance of the resurrection of Jesus for humanity in general and some aspects of its eschatological value and meaning.

The very nature and centrality of this subject for the Christian faith calls for serious reflection upon this event of God's activity in and with the world.

2. Some Poetic Reflections

1. The Significance of the Resurrection for Christians

In my view the resurrection of Jesus of Nazareth is not something that is simply a *consequence* of his work of redemption and reconciliation of the world in general and humanity in particular; it is a part of the work itself. The resurrection is not something merely designed to demonstrate Jesus' death on the cross to humanity, which the world scorned, but that it is the power and wisdom of God for reconciliation and redemption. It is not mere play-acting; it is itself power; it is itself wisdom. Moreover, in the resurrection of Jesus we have evidence of a love which will not suffer the life of fellowship with him to be destroyed or brought into meaninglessness or nothingness. This is just a sampling of the beginning of the significance or meaningfulness of Jesus' resurrection in the eyes, hearts, souls, and spirits of his early followers.

Evidence for this is articulated from the very beginning when on the Day of Pentecost the Apostle Peter made the following forthright, controversial declaration:

> "[...] this Jesus, delivered up according to the definite plan and foreknowledge of God, you crucified and killed, by the hands of lawless men. *But God raised him up*, having loosed the pangs of death, because it was not possible for him to be held by it. [...] Let all the house of Israel therefore assuredly know that God had made him Lord and Christ, this Jesus whom you have crucified." (emphasis added) (Acts 2:23, 24, 36)

We should also take note that the idea of resurrection was not something new for the followers of Jesus, i.e. it was not their creation. The Pharisees also entertained a view of resurrection, a position the Apostle Paul used effectively when he was placed on trial before the Sanhedrin. He shrewdly pointed out how natural it was that he, a Pharisee himself, would be tried for believing in resurrection. In this way, Paul was able to cause dissension between the Sadducees (who did not believe in an afterlife) and the Pharisees. And so we are able to see this concept was both current and controversial.

Regardless of the contemporaneousness or controversial nature of the idea of resurrection, or even of its historical roots, the Christian faith is grounded in this belief, i.e. belief in the resurrection of Jesus of Nazareth. It can reasonably be argued it was on this belief the church was built. While it is true this belief in a resurrection of Jesus cannot be scientifically verified or falsified, it may nevertheless be known, as was the experience of the disciples, existentially or experientially - and become for the believer an attested fact. Centuries later, the protestant reformer, John Calvin, would use the category of faith as knowledge to describe this concept.

What the resurrection faith did for the disciples was to reveal, to exhibit or manifest, to them the promise of victory over death having been fulfilled. It was their experience of union with the risen Jesus as the Christ which made them the persons they were. This experience brought with it a promise of Life, i.e. of an eternal life such as we find the Apostle Paul referring to when he wrote to his young friend Timothy:

> "[...] and now had manifested through the appearing of our Savior Christ Jesus, who abolished death and brought life and immortality to light through the gospel." (II Timothy

1. The Significance of the Resurrection for Christians

1:10)

Thus, according to Paul, we are taken out of the area of speculation and are confronted by the light, by the reality of the good news of the resurrection of Jesus, by the assurance that at the center of the cosmos, at the heart of all, there is One we may call Father, who will not forsake his children. Had Jesus not been raised our faith would be in vain; it would, at best, be as the unverified hope of the Pharisees, a hope without certainty and assurance.

It is significant that the Christian scriptures do not argue from a general to a specific resurrection. But rather, as the Scottish theologian John Baillie once argued, "the faith that Christ had risen (is) being made the starting-point of faith and that his saints will rise with him to newness of life." (Baillie, *And the Life Everlasting*, p.165)

2. *The Significance of the Resurrection for Jesus Himself*

With this brief introduction in mind, let us proceed to some aspects of the significance of this event of resurrection in a few specific areas, such as: for Jesus himself, for humanity, and finally its eschatological significance.

The Scottish biblical scholar and theologian, James S. Stewart, in discussing the issue of significance, notes how often the Apostle Paul uses the passive voice in preference to the active voice in connection with Jesus' resurrection. Thus Paul writes more frequently of Jesus *being raised* rather than *Christ arising*. This succinctly and clearly points to the strong belief that the resurrection was *God's act and God's authentication of Jesus as Messiah*. Paul sees a transition in Jesus from a state of *humiliation to exaltation*, an entrance in his risen humanity to new life of exalted power and sovereignty, whereby he becomes Lord of all.

3. *The Significance of the Resurrection for Humanity*

The resurrection also has its impact on humanity. In no part of Jesus' work as the Christ does he stand alone and in his resurrection, he takes the members of his body along with him. The believer, that is: the Christian, becomes a new person, a new creation in Christ, as we see in Paul's second letter to the churches of Corinth. In this relationship, Jesus as the Christ, is more than an object of faith, more than a type or model; in faith we are one with him. It was this experience of union with a risen Jesus that made (and makes) people who and what they are. We can then say that the epochal significance of the resurrection is: whereas in the *First Adam* we were given a living soul, in the *Second Adam*, who became a life-giving spirit, we may become a *kainei ktisis (a new creation)* and therefore walk *en kainoteiti zoeis (in new life and light)*.

In this new situation believers, according to Paul, possess the Spirit of Jesus the Christ which is the Spirit of God mediated through the exalted Christ that dwells in him. The Christian person, then, is a new person in Christ. It is in this experiential union with the risen Jesus as the Christ that we have the source and power of new life, of that new creation or new being. It is here, in this event, that we continue to experience the revelation of God upon which our new life as God's children rests. In other words, we are all children of God, not in the same manner as Jesus, but nevertheless, children of God.

Because Jesus as the Christ is the *pneuma zoopoiouv (the life-giving spirit)* we share in the risen life and become subjects of a moral and spiritual resurrection. As we participate in this marvelous and powerful event with the risen Christ, our newness of life receives its strength and nourishment. It is as we have the indwelling of his spirit that we have pardon and sanctification. As Paul speaking of himself put it in his letter to the churches of Galatia, "I live, and yet, no longer I, but Christ in me." (Galatians 2:20)

The resurrection may not in and of itself be the ultimate *parousia*, but it is significant in that *it is the First Easter. In this life-changing experience we can sense and feel the Love of God breaking into and shaping the present.* This idea was very prominent in the thought of Karl Barth, arguably, the most influential theologian of the mid-twentieth century. Barth summed up the foregoing thoughts in this way:

> "The third day of a new life of Jesus begins; but at the same time on the third day there begins a new *Aeon*, a new shape of the world, after the world has been completely done away with and settled in the death of Jesus, the Christ. Easter is the breaking in of a new time and world in the existence of the man Jesus, who now begins a new life as the conqueror, as the victorious bearer, as the destroyer of the burden of man's sin which has been laid upon him. In this altered existence of his, the first community saw not only a super-natural continuation of his previous life, but an entirely new life, that of the exalted Jesus Christ, and simultaneously the beginning of a new world." (*Dogmatics in Outline*, p. 122)

4. Some Poetic Reflections

I AM

(A poetic reflection on Exodus 3: 14 and Matthew 16:15)

I am the Rays of the Rising Sun,

Snow on the Mountains of the Moon,

The far-flung shadows of late afternoon.

I am the Wisdom of the sage.

I am the Refuge of all who weep.

I am the Mother of all who live.

I am the Promises I keep.

I am the One who sits with sorrow.

I am the One who feels your pain.

I am the Hope of your tomorrow.

I am the One who 'will' remain.

PRAYER

Lord Jesus, we give praise to you for everything which brings us
closer to you.

We lose all power, but we realize that your mercy
is sufficient for us.

We lose our good reputation, but we realize
your love is sufficient for us.

We lose all human support, but we realize
your word is sufficient for us.

We thank you for the glorious example of your love.

You believed in God even among unbelievers.

You obeyed God even among the disobedient.

You remained faithful to God even when tempted.

You loved us even when we betrayed you.

You helped us even when we hated you.

You save us even though we crucify you.

We admit we are afraid to confess you among those who laugh at you,

that we are ashamed of your poverty among the powerful;

that we are constantly tempted to reject your gospel

among the wise of this world.

We confess we more gladly serve those whom we like than those

who are strangers to us,

that we more willingly help those who are similar to ourselves

than those who are different,

that we prefer our friends to our enemies.

Lord, we thank you for the example of your Love.

We ask you to show us the way to the love which believes in you

even though it remains unanswered,

the love which serves you even if people do not

understand it,

the love which first seeks your will even if our

wills oppose it.

We ask you to show us the way to the love which sees in every

human being, the person

whom you love,

Part VI - The Resurrection of Jesus of Nazareth

for whom you died,

and whom you have forgiven,

and that thus we may see in every person those for whom you care.

Lord Jesus, grant that we may become followers of your example

 and servants of your kingdom and in the place where have put us.

Amen and Amen!

4. Some Poetic Reflections

Afterword

I have spent better than six decades exploring and visiting time and time again, many of the issues herein contained, as they continue to make their way into modern history. The past is always important and should play an important role in our religious faith, but that does not excuse us from joining in the challenges and diligently apply our faith understanding to the complex issues of our own day. This is what it means, in my opinion at least, to be a follower and ambassador of the Christian faith, but doing so in a spirit of collegiality with other persons of good will in order to make this world in which we find our ourselves a better, safer, and richer (not simply in the economic sense) place in which to live in peace and harmony.

Moreover, for me, if pressed to say anything more definitive, I would say that for the Christian faith, the one abiding factor which towers above all else is the one so beautifully summed up by the Apostle Paul in the closing line of his very famous *Hymn of Love*, (1st Corinthians, Chapter 13): *"Now abide these three: faith, hope, and love, but the greatest of these is Love!"*

This "Love", it seems to me, is found almost everywhere in the life, teachings, and commitments of Jesus of Nazareth, Who is the One we claim and call, the Christ. In a word: the very love of God was made manifest, in various and diverse ways, in his life, and this life presents us with a magnificent and noble challenge. It is, we might suggest, the acme of being *human*.

Many today, of course, are skeptics who claim that religious faith, of any type, including the Christian faith, are irrelevant. It seems obvious to me they have not read nor understood the meaning and significance of the Christian message (and other religious messages as well). I am always reminded of a wonderful book written by Dietrich Bonhoeffer many decades ago entitled *The Cost of Discipleship* (1937), in which he points out not only how significant and powerful the love of God for humanity is, but also how devastatingly "costly," if we take it seriously. Many adherents, he argues, such as the German National Church during the rise of the Third Reich, take the "easy" way out, that is to say, practice a "cheap, empty, meaningless form" of the grace Jesus so clearly and poignantly demonstrated to and for us. I sincerely hope we all shall do our very best to take up the serious and difficult challenges in our lives today (and they are many) - it will be, I believe, an amazing and rewarding experience so to do.

As always,
Pax et Caritas
Bill Anderson

Afterword